"Many of us are oblivious to th[...]ce.
Wes delivers insights into those challenges [...] f
creative, practical ideas for how we can minister to pastors and their
families. This book inspired me to bless my pastor and then told me
how. I'm eager to try out some of Wes's ideas."

—Ken R. Canfield, Ph.D., President, National Center for Fathering

"I believe that the ministry of 'encouraging pastors' is one of the most
neglected and needed today. Wes Roberts has been encouraging and
helping pastors for many years. His practical, spiritual insights will be
a help to all of us who desire to become more effective in encouraging
our pastors."

—Dr. Paul A. Cedar, President, The Evangelical Free Church of America

"All I can say is *finally*! The church desperately needs this book to
help their pastors navigate the turbulent waters of ministry."

—Roger Cross, President, Youth for Christ

"Books for and about pastors tend to fall into two categories: the ones
with the theory of what an ideal pastor should be and the ones that deal
with pastors as they are. This book falls into the second category, yet it
does not deny the nature of the 'heavenly calling.' Wes Roberts has
heard the personal cry of flawed human beings trying to carry the
responsibility of sainthood along with the expectations of lay people
who want the pastor to be a combination of all of the best of the edited
version of the media pastors while possessing the business acumen of
a Fortune 500 business leader. Roberts uses a broad range of real-life
illustrations and experiences gained in years of hearing both sides to
make workable suggestions to bring the ideal and the reality closer
together. Wes Roberts really cares about pastors and it shows!"

—Jay Kesler, President, Taylor University

"This long overdue book is packed with valuable insights and practical
suggestions that can make a significant difference in the life of your
pastor. *Every* congregation needs at least one copy."

—Gary J. Oliver, Ph.D., Clinical Director of PastorCare
and Missionary Care Services International,
author of *Real Men Have Feelings Too*

"*Support Your Local Pastor* should be on the shelf of every pastor and
in the heart of every elder and church member in the country. First,
Wes Roberts highlights the struggles and pressures of the modern-day
pastor. But he doesn't just leave it there. With great insight and creativity, he offers practical ways to honor those who've given themselves to
this special place of service in God's Kingdom. My advice to you is to
first read it, then *do* it."

—John Trent, Ph.D., President, Encouraging Words

SUPPORT YOUR LOCAL PASTOR

Practical Ways to Encourage Your Minister

WES ROBERTS

NAVPRESS

BRINGING TRUTH TO LIFE
NavPress Publishing Group
P.O. Box 35001, Colorado Springs, Colorado 80935

The Navigators is an international Christian organization. Jesus Christ gave His follow-ers the Great Commission to go and make disciples (Matthew 28:19). The aim of The Navigators is to help fulfill that commission by multiplying laborers for Christ in every nation.

NavPress is the publishing ministry of The Navigators. NavPress publications are tools to help Christians grow. Although publications alone cannot make disciples or change lives, they can help believers learn biblical discipleship, and apply what they learn to their lives and ministries.

Library of Congress Catalog Card Number: 95-38505
ISBN 08910-99239

Cover illustration: James Bozzini/Renard Represents

Some of the anecdotal illustrations in this book are true to life and are included with the permission of the persons involved. All other illustrations are composites of real situa-tions, and any resemblance to people living or dead is coincidental.

This publication is designed to provide accurate and authoritative information in regard to the subject matter covered. It is sold with the understanding that the author and the publisher are not engaged in rendering legal, accounting, or other professional service. If legal advice or other expert assistance is required, the services of a competent profes-sional person should be sought. *From a Declaration of Principles jointly adopted by a Committee of the American Bar Association and a Committee of Publishers.*

Unless otherwise identified, all Scripture quotations in this publication are taken from *The Message: New Testament with Psalms and Proverbs* by Eugene H. Peterson, copy-right © 1993, 1994, 1995, used by permission of NavPress Publishing Group. Another version used is the *HOLY BIBLE: NEW INTERNATIONAL VERSION*® (NIV®), copy-right © 1973, 1978, 1984 by International Bible Society, used by permission of Zonder-van Publishing House, all rights reserved.

Roberts, Wes.
        Support your local pastor : practical ways to encourage your minister / Wes Roberts.
        p.   cm.
        Includes bibliographical references.
        ISBN 0-89109-923-9
        1. Clergy—Office. 2. Clergy—Religious life. 3. Clergy—Family relation-ships. 4. Encouragement—Religious aspects—Christianity.
        I. Title.
BV660.2.R63   1995
253—dc20   95-38505
                                                                                 CIP

Printed in the United States of America

1 2 3 4 5 6 7 8 9 10 11 12 13 14 15 / 00 99 98 97 96 95

FOR A FREE CATALOG OF
NAVPRESS BOOKS & BIBLE STUDIES,
CALL 1-800-366-7788 (USA)
or 1-416-499-4615 (CANADA)

CONTENTS

DEDICATION

This book needs to be dedicated to all pastors everywhere. Ultimately, it is to honor each minister of the gospel of Jesus Christ that these words are written.

In bringing several names to this page of dedication, I look both back with gratitude on my own Christian walk and forward to the hope we can all have that there are some young men and women out there who are maturing well as ministers of the gospel.

Harold J. Westing was the first "real" pastor I knew personally. He was my youth pastor, many long years ago, whom God used to love me into the kingdom of God. This book is a result of your ministry in my life. Thank you!

Among the many pastors and Christian leaders it has been my honor and privilege to know around the world in recent years, the following men, younger than I, have allowed me to walk with them at a variety of sincere levels of friendship, at times as mentor, leadership coach, counselor, and spiritual director. All are points of relationship about which I have sincerely been so unworthy. But God has granted us special moments together, and I hope for many more. This one's for you, because I love you guys and thank God for you: Tom Albinson, Gary Bishop, Dru Dodson, Curtis Fletcher, Jeff Giles, Ken Glasier, Matt Heard, Scott Jackson, and John Swale.

ACKNOWLEDGMENTS

This has been both a hard and enjoyable book to write. It has been hard in that there is so much more to be said to us, the people in the pews, and to our pastors, on how to better care for, love, and support each other. This is certainly not an exhaustive grouping of ideas.

It has been enjoyable in that I have gleaned so many excellent ideas from so many fine people, which gives me hope for what is happening in our world in our churches. Being creative is a personal hobby — so this has been fun.

But I do need to thank a few good people in particular for their support and encouragement to get this project done. Those people are:

Steve Webb, Editorial Director at NavPress, is a true gem, a significant encourager, an excellent coach who knows what he is doing, a godly man with a deep heart, and if nothing else comes of this project, the friendship we have begun is a rare treasure for which I thank the Lord.

Dale Schlafer, Vice President of Church Relations for Promise Keepers, is a good friend whom God has used as both a Nathan and a Barnabas in my life. Right in the middle of consulting with him on the biggest ministry project either of us had ever undertaken, the 1996 Promise Keepers Clergy Conference in Atlanta on February 13-15 for seventy thousand clergy, he cheered me on to the finish line of this book. I know he prays for me daily—prayers and a friendship I do not want to be without. I thank God for him.

Those who have the correct, necessary, significant, and sometimes challenging task of holding my own feet to the fire are the members of the Board of Directors of the ministry I have led since 1982. They, and their spouses, have become one of the strongest communities of believers I have ever belonged to. They are godly, supportive, corrective, visionary, and just a little zany at times in all the right ways. I thank God for their belief in me and the ongoing work of Life Enrichment. May God bless Tim and Sharon Woodroof, Roger and Joanne Thompson, Dick and Bo Teodoro, Don and Danette Morgan, Marc and Marsha McBride, Gary and Jorie Gulbranson, Sandy and Bill Burdick, and Ron and Cindy Baldwin for their awesome and faithful support of Christian leaders worldwide.

I'm sitting here at the computer in my office with tears in my eyes—tears of intense gratitude for the wife and daughter God has given me. Judy, my bride since March of 1967, is one of the finest, most honest, genuine, fun, supportive, beautiful in spirit, and beautiful in appearance ladies you could know . . . and my best friend. Shannon, our wondrous daughter who came into our lives in April of 1976, is one of the most gifted, compassionate, bright, merciful, creative, curious, beautiful young women you could know . . . and my next best friend. I've put them through a lot, and still their love remains. There is no doubt I love them enough to die for either one if the need were that serious. In my thankfulness for each of them and for their love and forgiveness, I am thankful way beyond what mere words can express. I thank God for the sheer privilege of getting to live on the same planet with them day after day, laugh with them, cry with them, have them as family, daily pray for them, and watch God at work in their lives.

And to the awesome, holy, almighty, triune God: heavenly Father; my Savior and Lord, Jesus Christ; Holy Spirit, thank You for life itself, forever. Thank You for Your redeeming love and consistent grace. Thank You for Your convicting love and Your resurrection power. Thank You for Your call on my life to pastor pastors and other Christian leaders for the rest of my life. Lord, this is all so that Your glory, and only Your glory, will shine and be rekindled in the lives of men and women who are called to serve You in ministry around this world for years to come. Amen and amen!

IMPORTANT TO KNOW ABOUT THIS BOOK

This book is far from a solo effort. Over one hundred creative, caring men and women have contributed suggestions. Every member of the Life Enrichment Board of Directors, and their spouses, has sent in his or her thoughts. People from both sides of the pulpit have entered into this project from all kinds and sizes of churches from all sizes of communities, urban to rural. Simply stated, this book has been a delight to write with so much help, support, and encouragement.

Many of the good ideas suggested have given birth to other ideas. It has been a real treat to receive the variety of thoughts. It is a notable privilege to include the collective ideas of all these people in this book. To date, here is the list of those who have contributed their creative wisdom and insights. I wonder what a congregation would be like full of these folk?

A profound thank you goes to: Curt and Amy Anderson, Ron and Cindy Baldwin, Gary and Melody Bishop, Bob and Kathy Blume, Gail Bruntzel, Colin and Lorna Buckland, Rich and Linda Buhler, Bill and Sandy Burdick, Mark Carlson, Jerry and Ruth Collins, Greg and Sue Comfort, John and Jacque Coulombe, Jim Cummings, David and Kellie Damico, Dru and Jo Dodson, Mark and Karen Dossett, Todd and Elise Durell, John and Carol Elliott, Alex Embiridis, Dwain Fairwether, Curtis and Libby Fletcher, Steve Garcia, Bill Gerrity, Jeff and Pam Giles, Ken and Helen Glasier, Craig and Beryl Glass, Tina Green, Sandy Greene, Leroy Grimm, Gary and Jorie Gulbranson, Bill and Debbie Hambright, John and Mary Jane Hamilton, Matt and Arlene Heard, Wes and Crista Holen, Scott and Kim Jackson, JoAn Jacobson, Mark and Debbie Jevert, Allen Long, Marc and Marsha McBride, Dave and Karen McClellan, Hugh and Sherry McGowan, Forrest and Nancy Mobley,

Don and Danette Morgan, Don and Diana Neil, Dave Palmer, Hank and Sherry Pharis, Jay and Linda Riley, Judy Roberts, Rod and Marisa Rogers, James Ryle, Dale and Liz Schlafer, Herb and Sheila Shaffer, Dale and Melody Shantz, Charles Shepson, Bill Smith, Rick Smith, Roger and Jan Spoelman, Bob and Debbie Stauffer, Gary and Melissa Stewart, Dick and Bo Teodoro, Roger and Joanne Thompson, Paula Wanken, Harold and Betty Westing, Shawn and Terri Willoughby, Jeff Winter, Tim and Sharon Woodroof, and Wes and Linda Yoder.

An extra word of thanks needs to go to Linda Riley for allowing me to borrow generously from her excellent writing on the pastoral family. Portions of this book were taken from her publication *Esteem Them Highly: Understanding Your Pastor and His Family* (Called Together Ministries, 1987). Linda is a unique blessing to all of us who care for pastors.

If I've forgotten anyone, please forgive me. May God reward you—and everyone listed—with some extra blessings for your excellent contributions.

New ideas are always welcome. We all need to be consistently learning more about caring for our pastors. So if you have a better idea, a more unique suggestion, or a more gracious refinement of an idea contained in these pages, *please* send it to me for publication in our Life Enrichment newsletter, *Catch Up on Life*, or for a future edition of this book. That contribution will be deeply appreciated by all of us—especially our pastors.

Now we ask you, brothers, to respect those who work hard among you, who are over you in the Lord and who admonish you. Hold them in the highest regard in love because of their work. Live in peace with each other. (1 Thessalonians 5:12-13, NIV)

Remember your leaders, who spoke the word of God to you. Consider the outcome of their way of life and imitate their faith. (Hebrews 13:7, NIV)

CHAPTER

1

LOVING OUR PASTORS WELL

THE TIME: 9:37 P.M.

THE DATE: Saturday, July 29, 1994

THE PLACE: Boulder, Colorado—first row, left side—standing on the field of Folsom Stadium, University of Colorado, with my friend Dale Schlafer, Vice President of Church Relations for Promise Keepers.

THE EVENT: The concluding moments of Promise Keepers 1994. Coach Bill McCartney, founder of Promise Keepers, was calling all the pastors in the audience to join him at the foot of the stage for a prayer of honor and blessing on their lives. Over five thousand came down onto the field. Many were weeping at being cheered on by the remaining forty-seven thousand men. It was an electric series of moments I will never forget.

THE CONVERSATION: Behind me in the stands, two men were talking. From their look and style, I imagined them to be fairly successful business types. Most likely they were active in their own churches. Each wore a wedding ring, and looked to be of an age to have kids in high school or college.

It is not my normal habit to eavesdrop on conversations, but those two men and I, and 52,349 other men, were witnessing something of significance at that moment in time. The more they talked, amid the wild cheers that were being encouraged by Coach McCartney, the more I listened to their words. The conversation went something like this:

"I wish my pastor could be here right now."

"Yeah, me too."

"Does your pastor let anyone get close to him?"

"He did when he first arrived at our church. But as our church has grown he seems to have distanced himself."

"Our pastor's a great guy, but no one gets close to him either."

"Do you wonder what he would be thinking of what's happening here?"

"I think he would be scared to death, and yet want to be first in line, all at the same time. In our elder meetings he talks about feeling tired and lonely. But I don't have a clue about what to do to get close to him, except to keep praying for him—and that doesn't seem like quite enough."

"Sure wish my pastor were here tonight. He needs this. We need it together. We need more than just a huge mega-event like this. Sure wish I knew what to do for him. What will you do when you go home to honor and love the man?"

"I'm not sure."

"Me neither."

I am.

When those two words—three letters and a space: *I am*—showed up on my computer screen, my first thought was, *That could be interpreted as a little arrogant!* Maybe a better way to put it would be, *I do have some clues.* And I believe I really do, because for a growing number of years I have had the privilege of ministering to Christian leaders—especially pastors—who are hurting and in need of the kind of honor, love, support, and blessing those men I overheard were wishing they could more readily give to their pastors. That's the ministry God has called me to. Allow me to tell you more about it so you will have a better sense of where I am coming from in this book.

Since 1982 it has been my sincere privilege and distinct calling to lead a ministry dedicated to strengthening pastors, missionaries, and other Christian leaders in all their relationships:

▶ With the triune God
▶ In their marriages, families, and friendships
▶ With their boards, staffs, and constituents of their lifework
▶ In their leisure (more about this later)

Life Enrichment functions under the direction of a dynamic board of directors, with a small full-time staff, and with the welcome partnering of a growing number of other pastors, Christian counselors, professionals, and laymen who also have a deep heart for seeing individuals in leadership positions strengthened and encouraged. This "teamwork" happens through consulting, counseling, and conferences for individuals, boards, staffs, churches, mission organizations, parachurch groups, and professional and business people.

IN SUPPORT OF OUR PASTORS

If you could sit with us as the telephones ring each day in our offices and listen in on the conversations, you would possibly weep, most likely be startled, and often wonder what is happening to our Christian leaders today—even to the very best of them. To get a truly accurate picture, you would need to take at least thirty days to live night and day with your pastor (a rather scary thought for all concerned), your missionary friend, or that parachurch worker in whom you have an interest.

Unless you already are one, you may not know that being a minister in today's world has pressures that are sometimes hard to describe.

"So what?" you say. "My work has pressures too."

Of course! I know that. Life has more stress than we want to admit. But from my vantage point as a consultant to pastors and other Christian leaders around the world, I see people in ministry having some inherent burdens, pressures, and needs that other kinds of work do not have.

☞The lawyer can refuse to take on a client.
   The pastor may feel like refusing to see someone come
   into his congregation, but that is not his privilege.
☞The doctor can refer out to another doctor when it is best
   for the patient—or him.
   The pastor is not often prone to send people to another
   church, though he may be thinking that in tough moments.
☞The electrician can say, "I can't fix your problem for two
   days," and we can call the next service person on our list,
   who can come out right away.
   The pastor (even one who is wise with his schedule) is

on duty twenty-seven hours a day, thirty-nine days a month, 412 days a year. People seem to have no respect when they experience their emergencies, when they honestly need pastoral attention. At least the ones in our lives haven't been well scheduled.

I think (hope) you see the point. But just to make sure, I refer you to a survey of pastors by the Fuller Institute of Church Growth as reported by Dr. Arch Hart of Fuller Seminary at the Care Givers Forum at the Glen Eyrie Conference Center in Colorado Springs, November 7-10, 1991. Dr. Hart reported:

►90 percent work more than forty-six hours per week, and often more than sixty.
►80 percent believe that pastoral ministry is affecting their families negatively.
►33 percent say that "Being in ministry is clearly a hazard to my family."
►75 percent have reported a significant crisis due to stress at least once every five years in their ministry.
►50 percent feel unable to meet the needs of the job.
►90 percent feel they were not adequately trained to cope with the ministry demands placed upon them.
►40 percent report having a serious conflict with a parishioner at least once a month.
►70 percent do not have someone they would consider a close friend.
►37 percent have been involved in inappropriate sexual behavior with someone in the church.
►70 percent have a lower self-image after they've pastored than when they started.

WHY AM I SO TIRED?

The following lament comes from *Who Ministers to Ministers?* by Barbara Gilbert of The Alban Institute (page 3). The author is

unknown to me, but any pastor, in his weariest moments, will iden-
tify strongly with the poem's sentiments—no matter how experienced or inexperienced that pastor may be.

I am appalled at what is required of me.
I am supposed to move from sick-bed
 to administrative meeting,
 to planning,
 to supervising,
 to counseling,
 to praying,
 to trouble-shooting,
 to budgeting,
 to audio systems,
 to meditation,
 to worship preparation,
 to newsletter,
 to staff problems,
 to missions projects,
 to conflict management,
 to community leadership,
 to study,
 to funerals,
 to weddings,
 to preaching.
I am supposed to be "in charge"
 but not too in charge,
 administrative executive,
 sensitive pastor,
 skillful counselor,
 dynamic public speaker,
 spiritual guide,
 politically savvy,
 intellectually sophisticated.
And I am expected to be superior,
 or at least first rate, in all of them.

I am not supposed to be
    depressed,
    discouraged,
    cynical,
    angry,
    hurt.
I am supposed to be
    up-beat,
    positive,
    strong,
    willing,
    available.
Right now I am not filling any of those expectations very well.
I think that's why I am tired.

We wonder why pastors today are burning out at a faster rate than ever. The spiritual battles our church leaders face every day are not to be minimized in any way. In spite of all its significant rewards and blessings, the ministry is not what it used to be. A growing lack of respect for the pastoral position within our society is just one of several reasons why being in ministry has different pressures than twenty years ago.

The fact is, our pastors need our loving support or their chances of getting burned out, or even failing, are great. Scripture urges us to honor and care for our pastors. Consider the following passages:

And now, friends, we ask you to honor those leaders who work so hard for you, who have been given the responsibility of urging and guiding you along in your obedience. Overwhelm them with appreciation and love!

Get along among yourselves, each of you doing your part. (1 Thessalonians 5:12-13, *The Message*)

Appreciate your pastoral leaders who gave you the Word of God. Take a good look at the way they live, and let their faithfulness instruct you, as well as their truthfulness. There should be a consistency that runs through us all. For Jesus doesn't change—yesterday, today, tomorrow, he's always totally himself. (Hebrews 13:7-8, *The Message*)

The concern and challenge of this book is that we people in the pews wake up and smell the coffee: Realize that we—you and I—are in this world to do ministry together with our leaders. The apostle Paul wrote to the church in Ephesus that the pastor/teachers are called to equip the saints to do the work of the ministry. Guess who that is? It's us—you and me.

We are not to drain our pastors dry for our benefit. We are not to have relationships with them just to meet our needs, of which each honest, authentic person has more than his or her "fair" share. If we truly believe that the church is like a body, then those of us who are elbows. or kneecaps, or whatever, cannot forget to honor, pay attention to, and love those at the "head" of our local bodies (churches).

▶ These are our elders.
▶ These are our leaders—both paid and volunteers.
▶ These are the spouses of our pastors. It includes the kids in our pastoral families.
▶ Moreover, these are our pastors, both senior pastors and those in associate roles, both married and single.

Something must be done to encourage these individuals! And something is. I hope that is why you are reading this book.

We can read the two above portions of Holy Scripture in any version or translation, but the message is the same: You and I are to overwhelm our pastors with love and appreciation. Why? To encourage them to live faithful and truthful lives. There is profound mutual responsibility for all of us.

THOUGHTS TO PONDER

Our infinitely creative God has given us the capacity to think, feel, and reach out. He has put into each of us the potential to dream, reason, suppose, discern, and create. He has given us the gifts of our senses: taste, touch, sight, hearing, smell. He has given His Spirit to every man and woman, boy and girl who dares to be a whole-hearted follower of Jesus Christ.

Why did He give us all of these awesome gifts? Volumes have been written answering that question. Allow me to suggest two key principles.

First, none of us was created to live in isolation. Life does not happen in a vacuum. We were created to live in relationship—with God, with ourselves, with others.

Second, relationships are nurtured through expressions of love, honor, care, and concern. Supporting others takes awareness, time, planning, and creativity, getting to know the real needs and longings of another person.

The big question is: Why don't more people encourage their pastors? Here are a few reasons:

▶ Complacency.
▶ Lack of knowledge—how, exactly, do I do that?
▶ Thinking clergy don't need encouragement.
▶ Thinking what we do would not matter.
▶ Thinking we don't have the time, energy, money, or creativity to do something.
▶ Hoping someone else will see the need and do something.
▶ Disliking something about the pastor.

However, I say, with confidence, that you already have within you all you need to be of tremendous encouragement to your pastor and his spouse and family. If you are alive enough to be reading this, you are alive enough with God's gifts within you to extend His love and grace to others, creatively, in a way that will bring renewed hope, joy, life—not only to them, but to yourself as well.

What you may need is a nudge to get you personally engaged, to get responsible and take some action, in the middle of your own very busy life. Your gifts are unique. No one can do exactly what you can to love your pastor well. That thought leaves me with a warm measure of excitement for your pastor—and for you.

So, my friend and fellow pew sitter, read on, and consider yourself nudged by the wide variety of ideas in this book. Be open to the Holy Spirit's leading for just how creative you can be. Stretch yourself a bit and watch what happens with your pastors as they relax and come alive and move forward in their unique calling—ministers of the gospel of Jesus Christ. What an awesome calling. What an awesome task!

A FINAL WORD

From my observations of pastors and other Christian leaders over the years, I have categorized pastors' lives into three major areas of concern:

▶ Personal
▶ Marriage and family
▶ Ministry

I have further divided each major category into sections that will help you find some ideas to truly love your pastor. Take these ideas and put your own unique spin and twist to them. Some ideas will intentionally be repeated because we need to be reminded again and again of what we can do to support our local pastors in each of these vital categories.

Some ideas are so simple, so cost effective, that you may be insulted—"Doesn't he know I can think of that?" Well, good for you! When will you put your good ideas into action?

Other ideas are more elaborate. These take some "collective scheming" with a few other people in your congregation on how you are going to love your pastor to life—and not to death. Be willing to get others involved in the costs, the planning, and the activities. Make this a contagious effort within that particular body of believers you call your church home.

As you get ready to love your leaders in simple and creative ways, *be careful*. Be very careful of your motivation for doing what you will be doing. Be as practical or as lavish as you need to be.

But ask yourself this: Am I doing this as a demonstration of how much I love my Lord—and my pastor? Or am I doing this so that someone will think I am one incredible person? Pharisees don't make good lovers of others—doing what is right to do just for the recognition. Jesus had a few choice words for those folk.

Giving and getting any kind of a gift with a hook in it robs each person of the joy of living well in relationship. So check your heart. You may even want someone else to check it. And then get busy lavishly loving your leaders with your unique life-giving gifts.

One necessary and important word of caution: Good intentions can go bad. Men, you take the initiative and fully, creatively support the men in ministry in your church—and where appropriate, that includes the spouses and children of your church leaders. Women, take the initiative and fully, creatively support the women in ministry in your church—which includes the spouses and children of your pastors and other church leaders.

I know this can sound old fashioned, but be very careful—exercise wisdom—about the time spent "moving toward" a staff member of the opposite sex. Scripture says to avoid the appearance of evil. You may be thinking right now, "Hey, I'm safe I can handle it." And you may be right. But you may not know about the needs of the other person. I simply don't want to see our spiritual adversary misuse the intentions of your good heart, whether you are married or single, to any disadvantage. Godly caution concerning your relationships with valued members of the opposite sex is critical . . . vital . . . in order to truly care for your pastor with the freedom and grace our Lord requires of all our relationships.

I am trusting the Holy Spirit to lead you in this. Remember, it is Almighty God you are wanting to honor in how you support your local pastor(s). It is my sincere hope that you will be blessed as you are a blessing. Taking this word of caution to heart will allow that.

Let's covenant together to love our pastors well. Let's do it with creativity and sincerity. Let's have fun doing it together.

For the sake of the Kingdom.

For our pastors.

For our Lord.

2

PERSONAL LIFE
OF THE PASTOR

Several years ago, while consulting at a fine church in the north-central United States, I was startled to read a headline in the local newspaper, "Pastor Shot to Death in Own Sanctuary." This man had the daily practice of going into his church alone to kneel and pray for the people of his congregation. On this particular day he was late arriving back in the church offices for the weekly staff meeting. When one of his associates went looking for him, he was found shot once in the head on the stairs leading up to the pulpit.

What a tragedy. What a senseless act.

Though very extreme, I've run across too many clergy who might as well be shot dead, not from avoiding their call to be ministers of the gospel, but because some people in their pews are constantly taking other kinds of shots at them.

CLERGY KILLERS

I don't know specifically what fired up G. Lloyd Rediger, a pastoral counselor, author, speaker, and consultant from Minnesota who specializes in clergy leadership issues, but in the August 1993 issue of *The Clergy Journal* he wrote some strong and thought-provoking things about the reality of "Clergy Killers" in local churches. Rediger calls these people "CKs." The following quotation is reprinted by permission (copyright 1993 by Logos Productions Inc.).

> When I encounter such CKs I am reminded of biblical passages where religious people destroy or terrorize spiritual leaders. Even Jesus was not exempt.
>
> Nearly any experienced pastor and denominational executive has encountered these CKs. . . . We tend to deny, excuse or pamper them in the church. But because we believe such persons should not exist in the church, and that we should be kind and forgiving to everyone, we fail to admit or understand the tactics, motivation and devastating toll they take on the energy and resources of the church, besides the cruel damage they do to clergy and those dear to them.

CKs typically have intimidating power because they are willing to violate the rules of decorum and caring the rest of us try to follow. . . . CKs are masters of disguise. They can present themselves as pious, active church members who are "only doing this for the good of the church.". . . CKs have learned the power of throwing tantrums to get their way. They know how to be bullies. They know how to distract, confuse and seduce.

Cardiovascular disorders, cancer, arthritis, gastrointestinal disorders, respiratory problems used to be rather rare among clergy. And clergy used to generate the best mental health and longevity statistics of any profession. Not anymore. I hear of and work with highly stressed, paranoid, cynical, and dysfunctional clergy all the time now, with numbers growing. Many of these maladies are traceable to CKs and their effects. The costs to the church are enormous, in lost clergy, health costs, divided congregations, loss of ministry resources and in debilitated pastors unable to function at much more than a survival level. . . . More than one denominational executive has told me lately that as they travel across their district or the nation, they find attacks on clergy to be endemic.

The etiology of the CK phenomenon is not mysterious, for we have always had a few evil people in the church. But contemporary society is especially compatible for CKs. There is a general distrust of authority figures of any kind. There is biblical and theological illiteracy in the pews. This means many parishioners do not understand God's purposes and the dynamics of spiritual leadership.

There is a general attitude of entitlement growing in the church, in which church members feel entitled to comfort and privilege. And if a pastor does not please them, they are free to criticize and punish. There is a growing business mentality in the church which says that if the CEO (pastor) does not produce, he should be fired.

There is mobility among parishioners. This means that

they feel little loyalty to the "peace and unity of the church." For they will soon move on, without having to deal with the consequences of their irresponsible behavior. We are not training pastors to handle conflict, nor how to support themselves in survival situations.

All churches and pastors are not suffering, of course. And all critics of pastoral leadership are not CKs. But the killing of pastors is a serious, growing phenomenon. Some pastors are incompetent, and some "shoot themselves in the foot," but none of them deserves the torturing tactics of CKs.

Others support this opinion. The reality is that more messes exist than you can imagine, or would want to know. You may even be saying, "Good grief, Roberts. What a negative way to begin a book of help and hope." Guess what, I would agree. But on our way to hope, we need to get real with what *is* happening in too many places.

When I first read Rediger's article, I admit it pushed some defensive buttons in me. But the next phone call quickly dispelled whatever defensiveness I had mustered. It was from a young man seven years into his first pastorate. He said, "I don't know how much longer I can hang on. I'm just about dead, and so is my wife."

With heart aflame this young man had graduated with honors from a fine evangelical seminary. He was "lured" to a geographical area near where he had vacationed with his family as a child. A new church was getting started in a fast growing section of this town. He was winsome. He could preach well. He seemed to appeal to young and old. His would be the finest church-plant of the decade in his particular denomination.

About year four in this pastorate his dreams began to fade. He found out that the "new church" was really begun in reaction to the "old church" from which most people had come. Two babies in three years, and relatives clear across the country, began to take a significant toll on his marriage. Three CK couples emerged (don't be so surprised—every congregation has them) to hound his every move.

His responses were not good. His wife hid out at home, seething, taking care of the kids. He doubled his efforts to get every elder to evangelize two nights a week. He began to participate in "pity party" conversations with other pastors. Slowly his sermons began to preach his "points to prove" rather than the proven fundamentals of the faith of the gospel of Jesus Christ. The night before he called he had actually considered suicide, or running away. His character was at risk. His calling was in question. He had no personal community. And he had moved in three years from being a vital, competent pastor to the dreaded zones of incompetency.

What went wrong?

Who was to blame?

Is every pastor this personally troubled?

Allow me to tackle the second question first. Each of us needs to first be responsible for himself or herself. One of the biggest games in the world is finding someone to blame. After I had directed this young man and his wife to a Christian counselor who deals with a pastor's personal issues, and as I learned more of their story, I realized some things in their history, individually and as a couple, certainly contributed to this downward slide. Also, from a corporate perspective, no one had worked through the grief of the issues that had prompted a group of people to leave one church and begin another. If high hopes could get us anywhere, this combination of people seemed to be just about as good as it gets. But two pieces, of many, were glaringly absent: *honesty* and *prayer*.

On the side of this pastor, he felt a tremendous sense of isolation and loneliness, which I believe the enemy of our souls turned into a significant spiritual battle in his young life. In his particular denomination one did not admit such "weakness," nor any other potential temptation. He denied the depression and anger in his own heart and mind, often comparing himself to other church planters who were a little worse off than he. In the end, his conversations with his wife had become complaint jam sessions about "those people" in the church. And let us not forget he did have those CKs in residence.

On the side of the congregation, they made "doggone sure" that what irritated them at the "old church" was not going to happen at the "new church." In fact, they focused so hard on what "would not happen," that it did. And, of course, it was the new pastor's fault because of all his new ideas from seminary on how to worship and evangelize the unchurched. The cancer of "justified criticism" infected and whipped this congregation to a fever pitch. Some folks even left to start another new church, where they were certainly going to do things right this time.

Who was to blame?

Everyone, in some way, though each will find it hard to admit. All need to take "credit" in cases like this.

Now to the first question: What went wrong? Few were truly honest—beginning with themselves. Amazingly, when I was invited into this unique battle zone it was no surprise, yet quite a surprise, to find out that no one had ever prayed with another person about any of the pastor's or the church's issues. *Ever.* Churches that have a significant, rock-solid commitment to honesty and prayer among the members and for the pastor guard themselves against this kind of crossfire and destruction.

Let me repeat that in another way. Healthy pastors and churches are populated with a majority of people who are committed to honesty and prayer. Healthy pastors and churches allow the Spirit of the living God to work deeply in both their personal and congregational lives. Healthy pastors and churches (meaning the people in the congregations, no matter what the size or location) who are willing to be open, vulnerable, consistently interceding, who love and extend grace from a servant's heart, who make reconciliation and restoration a priority, will not be problem free (that status is reserved for heaven). But they will exude an attitude of enjoyment and encouragement and life from which our Lord Jesus Christ can be well reflected to each other and the world around us.

And finally the third question: Is every pastor this personally troubled?

Of course not. But every pastor is a "people," a sinner, just like you and me. And it's my hope that every pastor is committed to living in the grace of our Lord.

In our culture we are all prone to get caught up in the immediate. One of my favorite people on the planet, a man I am confident you would be thrilled to have as your pastor, a man of prayer and deep devotion to God, to his family, and to his people, recently wrote to me the following. I use it here with his permission.

> Change at the church is slow, but I am rejoicing in God's activity here. Last weekend we had over 200 show up for a vibrant time of prayer and fasting. God met us!
>
> On a personal level, I am hanging in there. Trying to get a handle on my schedule. I am also battling loneliness. I'm not connected with enough guys here and really lack a "soulmate" or two that I thought I would have by now. Please pray for that. Some of that reality is schedule related—translated: my fault for not making time. I am not leisurely relating enough, nor am I playing enough.

In the winter of 1995 I attended a conference at Glen Eyrie, The Navigator headquarters, and talked with a number of denominational leaders and others who minister to pastors. At one meal we were sitting around the table discussing a quote one man attributed to the pollster and researcher, George Barna: "Pastors are the most occupationally frustrated people in America." Another denominational head offered a quote he had heard from some major research, "Only four of every thousand pastors are doing highly effective work." All of us were in agreement on the four biggest issues that face a pastor today:

▶ Loneliness
▶ Inadequacy
▶ Family strains
▶ Financial issues

You may say, "Well, welcome to the real world." But for a person as public as a pastor, these issues can be addressed by those of us who sincerely care for the people who lead and shepherd us. The Bible uses the wonderful metaphor of shepherd and sheep when referring to us and the Lord, as well as those who lead us at church.

We may sometimes act as dumb as a sheep, but the metaphor breaks down in that we can think, and feel, and respond, and relate, and take, and give. It is in the giving category that we all need to improve, and can improve if we take the Word of God, the Bible, seriously:

> And now, friends, we ask you to honor those leaders who work so hard for you, who have been given the responsibility of urging and guiding you along in your obedience. Overwhelm them with appreciation and love!
>
> Get along among yourselves, each of you doing your part. (1 Thessalonians 5:12-13, *The Message*)

As usual, the apostle Paul is straightforward in his encouragement. This verse gives us — you and me, no one else — our "marching orders." Let's put on our creative caps and find ways to lavishly love, honor, and bless our pastors. Let's not expect someone else to do it. Let's not care who gets the credit. Let's be intentional with how we give this love away, this love that has been so freely given to us.

As you read through the following ideas on how to encourage the personal life of the pastor, don't forget that the topics of marriage and family life and ministry will follow. There will be some overlap, and there will be some repetition. But let us set our sights on loving our pastors — and all who minister on our church staffs — as they have never been loved before.

Do this, not just for their sake, but for Him.

PERSONAL ENCOURAGEMENT AND AFFIRMATION

Through Your Involvement in the Church

We are a society of spectators, and watching pastors has become a great game in Western society. We are also an incredibly busy society, and at church there is a tendency to "hire the ministry done." Consider the following techniques for involving yourself in your church.

GIVE TIME. You want to see a pastor faint? Take your pastor out to breakfast and tell him you have rearranged your personal schedule and—*shazzam!*—you have six free hours per month to give him in two three-hour blocks. If you gave him that time to help him with the life of the church, what would he want you to do? (Do not hold yourself to only the suggested time frame. Give more if you can. The concept of "under-promise and over-deliver" is crucial here if you really want to encourage your pastor.)

PRAY WITH HIM. Ask your pastor if you can come by the church once a month to pray with him for any need at the church, and keep at it consistently. Set the next month's prayer appointment before you depart this month's. Also, as appropriate to the situation, spread the news among the congregation to pray for the church and its critical needs.

THE VISION THING. Find out the vision your pastor has for your church, and if something also rings your bells, ask if you can help him champion that particular cause, in balance, with the rest of his vision for the whole church.

MOBILIZE AN ARMY OF VOLUNTEERS. "Where will we get the right church workers?" is one of the pastor's greatest worries. If you take the lead and, with your pastor's blessing, mobilize an "army" of people (don't forget what Jesus did with twelve disciples) who will keep all the volunteer slots filled in your church. Your pastor will nominate you first for sainthood someday—after he finds out this is not a dream but a God-blessed reality of care and concern from a person who truly wants to live out his or her involvement in a Christian community. If you want a great challenge and a good time of working with your pastor, this is it!

Simply stated, the best way to encourage your pastor personally in the life of the church is to get involved. Too many pastors feel various levels of defeat because they feel so alone in the ministry of the church. The more people who ask questions, show interest, and get involved, the easier it is to draw energy and to be motivated to keep going.

Through Relationship

GIVE HIM A CALL. With sensitivity to the pastor's schedule, give a spontaneous call to see how he is doing. Limit your call to five minutes or less, focusing on your care and concern. And do not say, "Now that I have you on the line, allow me to unload all my problems on you." Be single focused and brief with your word of blessing—it will be hard for him to believe you're doing it in the first place. Call back another time to tell him your troubles.

If he is busy, leave a message telling him he was on your mind and you just called to say, "I care about what is happening in your life today. You're in my prayers." What a boost just that much would be.

If your church has one of those newfangled voice-messaging systems, simply ask the secretary or receptionist to put you directly on the pastor's voice mail, and then leave your brief message. I know of one pastor who has yet to erase one message he received several months ago, it was of such profound and powerful encouragement to him. And it was only six sentences long.

TAKE HIM TO A SPECIAL EVENT. If there is a charity fund-raising dinner, auction or sporting event, special banquet honoring someone in your community, or an important benefit event coming up in your business and/or community social life, invite your pastor and his spouse to be your guests. Obviously you will pay their way—even for baby-sitting, if that is necessary. See if you can get a picture of you and them in the society pages of your town's newspaper. This says something solid to both your pastor and to your particular spheres of influence.

Along this same line, how about taking your pastor to a golf tournament with a couple of other men from your church, splitting his entry fee three ways? If he's not that good, give him a series of golf lessons beforehand, and maybe even a trip to the pro shop for new clothes to wear on the links. If he *is* that good, find out who his teacher is! Hang the "we gotta keep 'em humble" thoughts at a moment like this. We all enjoy feeling "first class" every once in a while. He will feel very valued and appreciated, and might even improve his game with the other pastors in town.

KEEP CONFIDENCES. Most pastors do not have close relationships in their churches because they fear (all too legitimately) that what they share will not be kept confidential, as in, "Do you know what I heard Pastor Webb say when he missed that putt at the golf tournament last week?" Seriously, it gets much worse. If we are honest, we must confess our fear of being judged and criticized. Therefore, if you should be so blessed with the confidence of your pastor and you break that confidence, may your tongue fall out— or worse. Even the simplest betrayal of a confidence shared does exceedingly great damage, at any place in our lives.

If your pastor takes the risk of sharing some part of his heart with you, make the assumption that it *is* in confidence, and that you can share what was said *only* if you ask him for permission. Otherwise keep the information to yourself and talk only to God about it, not even with your own spouse. Whew! If we all followed this one, there would be a new dawn of personal relationships with our pastors across our world—guaranteed!

BE HONEST AND DOWN-TO-EARTH. The best hamburgers in Colorado are tucked away in an old log-cabin pub at the end of a dirt road in the foothills outside of Denver. A great place to let down and talk, as a rushing mountain stream tumbles by. Since Jesus spent a great deal of time with publicans, tax collectors, and various other kinds of sinners, I would expect to find Him out there talking with people if He were to return today, especially given His penchant for being with people who needed Him most. Now, I am certainly not promoting bar-hopping, rather that you seek out that fun, unusual, offbeat, and yet safe place in your area. It's there somewhere. If you find the idea of associating with sinners in their element hard to swallow, relax. You're not there to participate in activities that go against your convictions. Just get that pastor of yours completely away from the usual routines of his life, and make it a vastly different place than he is used to. Be creative with what is in your neck of the woods. And of course, don't stretch the limits of his personal weaknesses or addictions—if your pastor is really overweight, don't do hot fudge sundaes. But how about a gentle stroll around the lake at your city park and a nice chat on a bench with you providing some ice-cold club soda?

Many pastors feel the aloneness of being regarded as out of reach or in some special category apart from the rest of the congregation. Most pastors deeply appreciate church members who can set that aside and talk shoulder to shoulder, eye to eye. Therefore, consider two places you're willing to "risk" taking your pastor in the next twelve months. Write them down now.

DO NOT STAND FOR GOSSIP. Whenever you hear people criticize your pastor, encourage them to go directly to him with those comments. In fact, offer to go along, not to dump on the pastor and put him in his place, but to bring the peace that understanding and the healing of relationship brings. As fellow believers in the gospel of Jesus Christ, we are all called to be peacemakers and ministers of reconciliation. *Do not* pass what you heard down the grapevine. That's gossip, and Scripture has some interesting things to say about that. You are not to be a telephone pole, but a conduit of God's grace in your relationships. What a difference you would make in your pastor's life if you would be mature and responsible enough to do that. I firmly believe God would rain blessings on you all. Critical people often think they do not have the leader's ear. Thus they talk among themselves, forgetting to read and follow the true and tested guidelines God has already given us in Matthew 18 to make things right with each other. It could be a novel thought to consider living biblically in our relationships with each other, and especially with our pastors. If you agree with what the other person is saying about your pastor, then make your own appointment and get things settled between the two of you.

STAND UP FOR YOUR PASTOR WHEN HE IS NOT PRESENT TO DEFEND HIMSELF.

NURTURE YOUR RELATIONSHIP WITH GOD. Seek the best personal relationship you can with God without being dependent on the pastor for how "spiritual" you are. Pastors are freed to be real in their own lives and to minister even better when they know that their parishioners are not solely dependent on them for their spiritual life. Your pastor would love to hear what you gleaned from your own time in God's Word (the Bible) this week.

TAKE A LONG WALK WITH HIM. Some pastors are real sports nuts — fishing, golf, running, etc. Others are not into that kind of "stuff." I've found that a long walk in an interesting and safe place is one of the best ways to hear the heart of a person, unless one is physically inhibited. It seems like Jesus did this a lot with those in whom He had a sincere and intense interest. Where would you like to invite your pastor on a walk in the next six months? And when will you make that date? Write your plans below.

Through Words and Notes

FORGET THE PRECONCEPTIONS. I have preconceived notions about every pastor I know, and so do you. Ask the Lord often to give you a word of encouragement for your pastor. Then listen with understanding to the word the Lord gives you — and not to your own preconceived ideas. Your pastor needs the encouragement that *only* you can give. And he needs it today.

SAY IT WITH A NOTE. If you were to browse in my office files, you would find one folder with handwritten notes, and even printed e-mail messages, that I have kept to read on down days when I have wondered if I'm fit to continue to serve within the kingdom of God. How about making a practice of sending your pastor a note of appreciation for something you've caught him doing very well? Taking the time and initiative to send along your compliments will be a tremendous blessing to your pastor. Do this at least every two months.

Along the same line, be bold enough to tell your pastor when the Lord used him to speak to you personally. Let him know when he has gotten it right from the Lord.

RECOGNIZE YOUR PASTOR'S GIFTS. Next time you see your pastor, look him right in the eye and say with sincerity, "God has really gifted you in (*choose one:* preaching, teaching, counseling, wisdom—whatever fits). It is good to see Him using you in that way." Pick only one area, though. That way you can make a different statement a month or so later. Be truthful, and don't gush. Also, stand by to help him up after he faints from your single, well-spoken compliment.

SPEAK THE WORD INTO HIS LIFE. Do it simply, and don't preach. Preaching is his job. Say, "Brother, 'Do not lose heart in doing good, for in due time we shall reap if we do not grow weary.' I'm praying for you!" Those kinds of thoughts can be either written or spoken.

SAVE THE SERMON COMPLIMENTS. You may think it a nice gesture to say to a pastor on the way out the door on a Sunday morning, "Nice sermon, Pastor." But that does nothing for him, really. Much, much better would be a letter from you arriving on his desk on the Thursday after the sermon—or even a month later. (Most pastors would be surprised and encouraged if you had remembered a message for that long.) Let him know just how and where that message got to you and what you have done about it. It is a human trait to be gripped, challenged, and changed by the spoken word, and then forget to let the speaker know just how much his words meant. A personal letter is sincere appreciation of the highest order. Jot down the last idea you got from your pastor that the Holy Spirit used to impact you in some profound way, and let your pastor know about it soon—in writing. In fact, do it now. We've provided the space.

KNOW WHEN NOT TO WRITE. If you find you have a difference of opinion with your pastor, *do not* let him know that in writing. Written criticism is not biblical and is senseless. There is no opportunity for dialogue and making peace with the situation. Written words, used in this way, become arrows that kill the spirit. Talk it out—soon. That is God's way.

SAY IT WITH A CARD. I am a great believer in sending cards of encouragement to people, both handwritten and preprinted. DaySpring Cards, available at your local Christian bookstore, is doing a phenomenal job of helping all of us appreciate our pastors. They have cards both serious and funny to get our love across to our pastor, his spouse, and others on the church staff. Run—don't walk—to get a handful of these.

The division of Ministry to Pastors of Focus on the Family is also doing a splendid job of making us all aware that October is "Pastor Appreciation Month." Call them for one of their "Pastor Appreciation Kits." But surprise your pastor and make him wonder what you are up to by personally choosing another month of the year to also honor him.

OR EVEN A GIFT. Instead of a card or a letter of appreciation, you may want to purchase an object or symbol that shows your appreciation and deliver it with a note—either in person or anonymously. A friend knew that his pastor was impressed and moved by a fine art print he saw at a local Christian bookstore. So he went and purchased it. Then he asked the church custodian "secretly" to let him into the pastor's study several weeks later and hung it on the wall, with nothing more than a simple scrawled note—*no* signature—saying, "Pastor, you need to know there are people in this congregation who are for you and love you." That note is still taped to the frame of that picture in that pastor's study for all to see. What a testimony of genuine love and honor! I can tear up just thinking about the resulting impact it has had on one fine pastor and a congregation.

Through Prayer

PRAY FIRST. Pray for your pastor first—not as a last resort.

PRAY OFTEN. Commit to praying for your pastor or pastors regularly, and let them know you are doing that. Tell them you will be praying for them every Tuesday—and just do it. They will probably be praying for you, too. And then, on the occasional Tuesday, send them a note to let them know what you prayed about for them. What encouragement!

Better yet, pray for your pastors every day, asking the Lord to keep the adversary of all our souls away from them.

PRAY AS A TEAM. If you are one of those people who is a true intercessor, how about organizing a pastoral prayer team (which doesn't mean getting your pastors together to pray) to lift up your church staff daily to the Lord? People have committed to praying *at least* one day a week for our ministry. During hard moments, I often get reminded by the Spirit of God that someone is praying, which becomes a powerful uplift.

USE A CALENDAR. Develop a prayer calendar for the people in your church and pray for a different staff person with a particular need every day of the month. Include staff spouses and kids. Let the staff family members know with a note or call what you prayed about for them.

PRAY FOR THE WHOLE INDIVIDUAL. Be committed to praying for all the facets of your pastor's life, and ask your pastor what you could pray for in each of these areas:

▶ *Spiritual*—Does he need a fresh touch from God?

▶ *Emotional/Intellectual*—Does he need extra wisdom and understanding?

▶ *Physical*—Does he need encouragement to get in shape and stay there? To take better care of himself nutritionally?

▶ *Marriage/Family*—How could you sincerely pray for his kids? His spouse? You can even ask the spouse how you can pray for both of them and their kids. (A word of warning here: They may not believe you will really do that, but just do it and leave the results up to our Lord.)

▶ *Social/Fun/Friendship/Time for Relaxation*—Let your pastor know, with sincere warmth and love, that you are asking God to bring great conviction to him if he does not take all of his day off to get refreshed and renewed so that he can love his family better and be a growing minister. This would be a new word of encouragement: "Pastor, when you go on vacation next week, I'm going to be praying that you and your spouse and family have some times of great laughter. So be ready for the Spirit's blessing in this way!"

▶ *Financial*—Don't just pray about your pastor's finances, put some feet to your prayers. Ask God what needs to be done to make certain all of the financial needs of your pastoral team are fully met, and take those thoughts and concerns to your church board.

▶ *Vocational*—Ask your pastor, "Since we are in this ministry together, what are the three items that are heaviest on your heart as you lead us that need prayer right now? Today? This week? This month?"

GIVE A BOOK. If you are sincerely interested in praying for your pastor, Peter Wagner's book *Prayer Shield* will give you significant insights. In fact, you will glean ideas about praying for all the

Christian leaders in whom you have an interest. Glen Martin and Dian Ginter's books *Power House: A Step-By-Step Guide to Building a Church That Prays* and *Drawing Closer: A Step-By-Step Guide to Intimacy with God* would also be helpful.

Through Acceptance

GET THAT PASTOR DOWN OFF THE PEDESTAL YOU HAVE PUT HIM ON. Sincere respect and admiration is one thing, but placing pastors on pedestals is courting disaster, for there is not much room on a pedestal. These are regular folk, called and anointed by God for a particular purpose in this life, just as you are in your own places of service to the King. Allow your pastor to be human—pastors are a lot more believable that way. They have struggles, even if they pretend they don't, and they are often tempted in the same ways you are. You need to remember that they get frustrated with the garbage disposal in the kitchen sink, and with the car, and have lawn mower problems just like everybody else. They have to face such things and still preach with integrity on Sundays.

LET THE PASTOR INTO YOUR LIFE. Let him know about God's work of grace in your own life, where you have failed, and how you have been pulled back from the brink of disaster by the hand of almighty God. He will feel less inclined to remain on a pedestal.

LET THE PASTOR'S FAMILY BE FREE. This is a hard one, but you can handle it or you would not be reading this book: Don't require your pastor's spouse or children to fit into a certain mold. Do all that you can to let each of them be uniquely who they are. If the preacher's kid has longish hair and an earring, smile and remember what kids did in your day (we rolled up our T-shirt sleeves to be cool—it sure looks dumb now). There are worse things that could be happening. Don't judge. Fads come and go, and some even recycle.

ALLOW YOUR PASTOR TO BE ONE OF THE GUYS. One group of men does "boys' night out" through what they call the GTC (Guy

Thing Club). They recently gave their new pastor a grand initiation into the club. They didn't ask him if he wanted in; they just told him, "You're in!" When they are out, no talk about any of their workplaces is allowed—including church. If their plans get a little grandiose, they charge the pastor twenty dollars and split the remainder of his costs between them. They even have a serious retreat or two each year to talk over the heavier "guy things" in their lives, plus they go to a Promise Keepers stadium event for men in a different city each year. Talk about something good, for each other and for their pastor. The wives love those guys holding each other accountable. And the pastor's wife says she has never seen her husband so energized.

ENCOURAGE HIM TO HAVE FRIENDS. Pastors need to be encouraged to have friends who will love them for who they are and not for their ministry or accomplishments. Many pastors are extra gunshy on what it means to have and/or be a friend because they have been betrayed or misused. Try this one on for size: With all due respect to the pastoral role, the next time you introduce your pastor to someone simply say, "I'd like you to meet my good friend, Gary Bishop" or "I'd like you to meet one of the best fly-fishermen I know. This is John Seville" or "I'd like to introduce you to Curtis Fletcher. He has a very creative mind." Think of three different ways you could introduce your pastor that would not give away what he does but would make a good statement of who he is. Leave it up to the other person to find out what he does. Jot down some of those words of introduction right now.

Through Humor
ELICIT FUNNY MINISTRY STORIES. There is not a pastor alive who does not have funny stories about being in the ministry. Ask

your pastor about his. If you need some categories, try these: baptisms, weddings, funerals, baby dedications or baptisms, church picnics, sermon bloopers, most embarrassing moments. Such stories *are* out there. Be prepared to laugh your head off with him, and a great time will be had by all!

START YOUR OWN GAG SERVICE. A man who has been a faithful usher for years hands the pastor a new joke each week before he goes into the morning service. Talk about great expectations, and consistent love and care. Most Sundays that pastor arrives on the platform with a true smile on his face. What a gift that usher gives. Another technique: Send your pastor an occasional cartoon you think he will enjoy.

KEEP THOSE CARDS COMING. Humorous cards should lighten most pastors' loads for a moment or two. I make it a point to hit a card shop about every six weeks to stockpile humorous and creative cards for when the need arises. You could do that as well.

SHARE A MOVIE. If you have seen a funny movie or video, take your pastor and spouse to see it. Or rent the video for them. Or even ask the church staff over to your house for their weekly meeting and show the video to them—with popcorn, of course.

DON'T LET YOUR PASTOR TAKE HIMSELF TOO SERIOUSLY. Be gentle and tasteful when you do this—not embarrassing in any way—but playing a fun, practical joke can let anyone know he is loved well. On your pastor's birthday, hang a big banner from the church that declares "Our pastor is fifty-one years old today!" Or figure out how to get a message on the Sony Jumbotron at your local ball park: "The congregation at Berean Baptist Church wants the world to know that we have the greatest pastor, Roger Thompson!" Or do the same thing with a half-page ad in your local newspaper. If your pastor enjoys crazy stunts, you could all show up in shorts on a hot summer Sunday, but ask his wife to bring him a pair of shorts to change into. What would be fun to do to, with, or for *your pastor*, or his spouse or family?

PERSONAL DEVELOPMENT

Through Accountability

ENCOURAGE AN ACCOUNTABILITY GROUP. One close pastor friend wrote me the following. I use it here with his permission.

> Accountability does not mean just giving an account about ministry or talking flippantly about different things. But it is giving an account about personal places in my life with a few good men whom I can trust completely. I need these men to ask me the hard questions and confront me about real issues in my life and ministry. In avoiding this I found it to be a wall of protection in my life. I found that many times it is difficult to open up and be vulnerable for fear of rejection and because of what people are going to think. It was something I had to overcome in order not to repeat some of the mistakes I had been making in my personal life, my marriage and family life, in some friendships and in my ministry. And I needed to be accountable to some men, not just my spouse, but to other godly men who would love me, be objective, could be trusted, would be true friends. Three men in our congregation dared to pursue me for a number of months for just such a purpose, waiting patiently for me to let down my barriers. They have been God's greatest gift to me in this ministry. To date, they have not broken a confidence, and they regularly hold my own feet to the fire on my own life issues. If God ever wants me to leave this church, He is going to have to move four families all at the same time.

I would recommend that each leader on your church staff have at least three people (men to men and women to women) who regularly meet and pray with him. The pastor can simply make a covenant to be accountable to them for his personal and ministry life. The church board would know who these people are and would pray for them in their unique ministry of support to the staff person.

Challenge the pastor to give the group permission to speak truth into his life no matter how painful it is. They need to have the "right" to enter each other's "space" unbidden.

These should be mature, godly, serious, fun-loving people who are not given to control, are not codependent, and are not newcomers to the congregation. They *must* have the confidence and trust of the pastor! And they must pledge confidentiality. They will not talk to members of the church board or anyone else *unless* they find criminal activities, suicidal behavior, or sexual misconduct. In cases where they feel they must go to the board, other church authorities, civil authorities, the spouse, etc., they pledge to speak to the pastor first, to give him an opportunity either to go with them or before them. These will be people who will "hang in there" no matter what.

I would suggest that they *not* be members of the church board, however. That promotes conflict of interest, and mixes up the intentions of two necessary groups of people around the pastor.

It takes time to build a group like the one mentioned above. But let your pastor know that you are praying for him to find friends with whom he can be himself and be fully accountable as a person, apart from his role as a pastor.

CLERGY SUPPORT GROUPS. Sometimes it is simply best to encourage your pastor to find other pastors in the community or denomination with whom he can be accountable. Ask him to look into it, and do all you can to help make it happen.

MEET SPIRITUAL NEEDS. Ask your pastor what time and resources he needs in the next six months to help his spiritual growth, then do all you can to make that happen within your congregation.

SEND THE PASTOR AWAY FOR A WEEK. One honest pastor wrote, "Balance—this is probably the issue I've struggled with most. Because I love people and I love what I do, it's tough for me to get and maintain a balance with family, work, emotional, physical, and spiritual health. Every part of who I am affects my work, and I long for my people to realize that for themselves and for me and my staff."

Would you be willing to champion this thought in your congregation? Send each of your pastoral couples on a week-long trip every three to five years. This will allow them to check on their health in all dimensions of their lives. Don't count it as vacation time, study leave time, or a mini-sabbatical, but as a gift of love from the congregation to make certain there is balance in each couple's relationship and in what they are called to do. Refer to chapter 6 for more resources.

Through Books

GIVE GIFT CERTIFICATES. The sight of a bookstore beckons most of us to come in. How about encouraging your pastor with an occasional gift certificate—but with a twist? One time let him know the certificate can be used only for books on his favorite hobby, another time encourage him to buy a book for his spouse, another time tell him it has to be a novel, another time a ministry book. This is a great way to help your pastor stay current with what is available in various areas.

PUT UP A READING CHALLENGE. A parishioner who is gifted in reading could challenge the pastor to read two books per year, and the two could get together to discuss the content. Or you might encourage your pastor to read a book along with you, one chapter every week or two, and then get together to discuss what was meaningful to both of you.

GIVE BOOKS. If your pastor is interested in history or spiritual direction, there is a fascinating series of six novels by Susan Howatch on the Church of England, beginning with *Glittering Images*. Eugene Peterson has also written an excellent trilogy on ministry that would be very helpful to your pastor: *Five Smooth Stones*, *Working the Angles*, and *Underneath the Unpredictable Plant*. Read these first and then discuss the content with your pastor. These will help you understand what it is your pastor is called to do as a minister of the gospel. Also, you can't go wrong with humorous books.

GIVE MAGAZINES. Ask him what magazines he would subscribe to if he had some extra funds—then subscribe for him. Or tell him you want to pay up his subscriptions for the next two years for his three favorite Christian magazines, and then get ten other couples at church to help.

GIVE BOOKSHELVES. Make certain that your church staff has very nice, sturdy bookshelves in their offices and in their homes. If you can't do the work yourself, find a carpenter, cabinetmaker, or handyman in your church who can (ask others to help pay for materials). Make it a project of the men in your church. It doesn't take a whole lot of talent to stain the shelves (that's where you would find me on this mutual project of care and love).

GIVE THE WORD. Buy him a new Bible of his choice if you notice his old one falling apart in the pulpit each Sunday. Better yet, offer to rebind the old one—all of his study notes, written in the margins over the years, are hard to give up.

Through Health
SEE TO YOUR PASTOR'S FITNESS NEEDS. How about asking your pastor if he would like a family membership to a health club? If he would, take care of the details. Make certain it is to a place of his choosing and not just your favorite club. If your church is really serious, *provide* the health club membership as a part of the pastor's basic package. Word will get around, and you won't have to hunt for good staff.

One Sunday school class in a fair-sized church gave their pastor a series of appointments with a personal trainer for a year when they became concerned with his physical condition. Talk about accountability week after week! Speaking of accountability, allow you and your pastor to be answerable to each other for your exercise programs. Doing something together will be extra good for both of you.

Another great outlet for exercise and fellowship for you and your pastor is church sports teams. You don't even have to be good to enjoy the benefits.

WALK WITH HIM. Give your pastor a pair of quality walking shoes and six pairs of white socks and let him know you want to walk with him at least three mornings per week.

SEE TO YOUR PASTOR'S HEALTH NEEDS. Check with your church board to make certain the staff is getting annual physicals. Men, stereotypically, avoid going to the doctor. Also, make certain your church staff has the best in health care insurance. Don't skimp here, for one never knows when this will be needed. It is a tremendous way of saying, "We really do care about you in all ways."

DEALING WITH THE PASTOR WHO NEGLECTS HIS HEALTH. How do you talk to someone who shows little concern for his health? Carefully, and with the confidence that a relationship can build over time. Whether the issue is excess weight, stress, nutrition, whatever, be extra sensitive here. There are often emotional reasons out of an individual's personal history for physical neglect. I'm talking about a situation that is obviously serious. Pray for the moment when this can be addressed, man to man, if the Lord keeps laying this concern for your pastor on your heart.

LEISURE

Non-Church-Related Activities
MAKE CERTAIN EACH PASTOR IN YOUR CHURCH TAKES HIS FULL DAY OFF.

GIVE A MONTH'S VACATION. You may disagree with me, but if you gave me thirty minutes of your time I think I could convince you without too much trouble to give each of your ministry staff one month's vacation per year. You may suggest that they take two weeks in the first half of the year and the other two in the second half. Spread it out. You may also urge them to take one of those weeks alone with their spouse—no kids at all. Do what you can to help this happen with your pastors.

REMIND YOUR PASTOR THAT HE NEEDS REST. This helps give him permission to take it. God created a Sabbath rest and required His people to use it up weekly—not to store it up annually (are you listening for yourself here?). God gave this rest with divine purpose and as a divine edict, not as an option. Our VCRs and phones have "pause" buttons. Remind your pastor to push his weekly.

PROVIDE A PLACE FOR R AND R. If both you and your spouse work, and you have a nice home with a quiet backyard or garden, offer it to your pastor as an occasional refuge for rest and reflection while you're at your jobs. Leave out some healthy treats for him.

ALLOW YOUR PASTOR TO PLAY. In fact, encourage him to take time for himself—to golf, fish, walk, do woodworking, go to the movies, attend a ball game—on days other than his day off. Also, find out your pastor's recreational interests and give him a gift certificate so he can splurge a little on himself. Encourage him to do something with no redeeming social value, something he has been wanting to do just for the fun of it. If there is cost, provide the funds.

ENCOURAGE A HOBBY. Find out what your pastor's interest or hobby is, and do something to encourage it. If the pastor is interested in astronomy, fishing, painting, or whatever, he will be most pleased to experience or have something new in this area.

HELP HIM CHANGE HIS ROUTINE. We all need to do something to change our routines. See what your pastor would like to do, explore, or learn to change his routines, and help him do it.

ENCOURAGE YOUR PASTOR TO JOIN ROTARY OR SOME OTHER SERVICE CLUB. This is a fine way to further the impact of your church in the community and to spend some time with your pastor.

HAVE A PASTOR OVER FOR THE EVENING. Invite your pastor and spouse over for the evening with no agenda other than just to be with them — and let them know that.

TAKE HIM TO A FUN PLACE. Almost every Christian leader who has visited us over a weekend has gone with us to a great place in downtown Denver called ComedySports. It is good, clean comedy improvisation by a group of incredibly talented people. We have laughed, had great fun, and been just a little crazy with all these dear people, some of whom are recovering from past wounds. Most pastoral couples don't laugh enough. Think hard: Where could you take your pastoral staff just to laugh and be silly? Or what kind of party could you throw to get your church staff laughing again — or at least more than they do now?

THE LITTLE THINGS

That Help Financially

DO AN ACT OF KINDNESS WITH YOUR CHECKBOOK. You could anonymously pay a utility bill or some car-repair bill you know he has. Or buy things you see he needs but may not be able to afford (like four new tires for his car).

Or try this: Ask to borrow the pastor's car, take it and have it completely detailed, then take it back with a full tank of gas.

GIVE SOME MONEY TOWARD TUITION. Do this if the children of the pastor are in a private school, but don't let him know who did it.

DO SOME ACT OF KINDNESS IN THE OFFICE. Do the pastors have all they need in their offices? Is the equipment less than three years old? Do your pastors have the computer equipment they need? How about comfortable and ergonomically correct office chairs to prevent backaches? Are their desks and chairs the right height? Is the furniture nice—or does it look like it was left over from the Civil War? Do they have room in their offices to meet confidentially with people? Are their studies private enough for reflection and prayer? Are they well painted and the carpet as new as possible? Do you have the carpets cleaned at least annually? Have you ever had a lighting expert and an office interior designer evaluate your church offices to make recommendations for what would improve the day-to-day working environment in color, lighting, room arrangement, etc.? Are the offices adequately heated in winter and cooled in summer? If the church offices have windows, do they work correctly? If your church office space is not the best, are you providing adequate offices elsewhere so that the "work" of the ministry can function well? Do your pastors have a study/retreat in their homes to get away to?

To all these questions—if not, why not? Begin the necessary funds and/or programs to bring solutions to these needs.

GIVE YOUR PASTOR PROFESSIONAL PERKS. What is your profession? What skills do you have—tax preparation, medical, dental, handyman, home repair, car repair, golf or skiing lessons, gardening? Offer them free to your pastor in a one-time or lifetime deal. Also, if your business provides special benefits for employees, and it is ethical and economical to do so, include your pastoral team on such things as discount privileges, etc. Share whatever you can from your own profession or business with your pastor—not just the leftovers.

LOAN THE PASTOR A SECOND CAR. Whenever you are out of town, take your second car over to one of your pastors to use. It would just sit in your garage anyway. Why not help out one of your pastors who may be lacking transportation?

PLAN FOR YOUR PASTOR'S RETIREMENT. Make certain your church has a more than adequate pension or retirement program for your pastors. Most churches I'm aware of fall short in this area. Retiring then becomes a very dishonoring event as those dear saints struggle to live out their days. Aging pastors have often given so much of themselves away over the years that they have not paid attention to the future in this way. Commit to paying attention for them.

REJOICE IN YOUR PASTOR'S POSSESSIONS. If by some stroke of blessing your pastor has something nicer than you, rejoice with him. Don't snub or envy him.

That Make Life Less Stressful

This series of ideas could fit in the chapter on marriage and family, but with some intentionality I put it here. So often the personal stress a pastor faces is in some of the mundane chores that chase us all. Enacting some of these ideas will significantly help him have time for himself and his family.

LOVE HIM, LOVE HIS CAR. Wash your pastor's car in the church parking lot sometime. To modern man, it is as close as you get to foot washing without removing the socks.

Or you might want to service his car for him. Why do we let our pastors run around town in cars that drip oil and look like they made a dozen laps at the demolition derby? How about seeing that regular maintenance gets done? Or in parts of the country where harsh winters or sea air do damage, how about rustproofing or winterizing the pastor's car? His prayers will be answered when you ask to help—unless of course, car maintenance is his hobby and/or your vocation.

Or be totally radical and help the pastor learn to maintain his own car. Most of these guys know Greek and Hebrew but zip about car maintenance.

REDUCE HIS STRESS. Take the risk of asking your pastor what three items or activities bring him the most stress in his personal life, and then attempt to reduce that stress or take it away.

HELP AROUND HIS HOUSE. Offer to help him with some job that needs to be done at his home to allow him more time with his family, such as mowing his lawn or painting. Arrange for the men of the church to paint his house on two consecutive Saturdays, and make certain you check with his wife on the colors.

HELP AROUND HIS YARD. On his day off, the last thing a pastor probably wants to do is prune trees, cut grass, trim hedges, and clean up. Offer to bring in a crew to do it all so he can select his "rest of choice" for his day of rest and leisure. This is a wonderful way to show that you do care for his well-being.

PROVIDE A WINTER'S WORTH OF FIREWOOD—CUT, DELIVERED, AND STACKED. Ignore this tip if you live in Hawaii.

ASK YOUR PASTOR WHETHER YOU COULD RUN AN ERRAND FOR HIM.

RESPECT YOUR PASTOR'S PRIVACY. Give your pastoral families an undisturbed dinner hour between 6:00 and 8:00 P.M. Don't call before 7:00 A.M. or after 10:00 P.M., except in true emergencies. Use directory assistance or the church directory rather than calling the pastor at church or home for phone numbers of fellow parishioners.

And, very important, *do not call the pastor on his day off.*

ON SHARING GIFTS. If you have gifts to share with the pastor's family, consider giving them through the pastor so that he will receive honor in the eyes of his family.

That Are Just Plain Fun and Simply Say You Care

CELEBRATE YOUR PASTOR'S ANNIVERSARY. Creatively find some way to mark the anniversary of when your pastor came to your church, either on the very day or on the weekend closest to it. Be creative from year to year. Here are some suggestions:

▶ Send him a thank you card shower.
▶ Send him flowers.

▶ Put a notice in the town paper with an article reporting how beneficial he has been to the church and to the community.

▶ Give your pastor and spouse a weekend away at a charming bed and breakfast inn.

▶ If it's a Saturday, sneak over early in the morning with breakfast. Call or knock first.

▶ Take your pastor's kids home with you for the night and leave your pastor and spouse at home with dinner catered in and a basket of breakfast goodies. Don't forget to include candles and bubble bath.

▶ If it's a special anniversary, like ten, fifteen, twenty, or more years, then pull off a surprise "This Is Your Life" event detailing God's blessing in the life of the church and the life of this dear person.

▶ Send the pastoral couple to the big city for a weekend with transportation, hotel, meals, and theater tickets all purchased ahead of time.

▶ Hang a banner across the front of your church, telling the world how much you love your pastor for his years of service.

▶ Board members' wives could throw a special luncheon honoring the pastor's wife. And just for fun, make it like a bridal shower.

▶ As an individual, bring your pastor one treat every day on the days leading up to the actual anniversary of his arrival—nine years, nine days, nine treats, for example. Make a game of it, leaving your little surprises without getting caught. Ideas: a bag of his favorite jelly beans; a coupon to a car wash; a half pound of flavored coffee; a can of new tennis balls (if he likes tennis); a certificate for two at his favorite Chinese restaurant; a coupon for a haircut with his barber; one-half of a fifty-dollar bill, with a small treasure map indicating where to find the other half (believe me, he'll go looking for it!); a six-pack of his preferred soft drink; the newest book by his favorite author—you get the idea.

But while I think about it, why wait for anniversaries? Do something just because it's Tuesday and you really do love that pastor of yours. Pick one for this week, for the fun of it, and just do it!

REMEMBER OTHER SPECIAL DATES. How about remembering in some manner the birthdays and wedding anniversaries of your pastors and their families? Release your pastors from any "duty" on their kids' birthdays and on their wedding anniversary. In fact, insist that they do nothing church related on the days when they can celebrate these important moments with family members.

FLOOD YOUR PASTOR WITH LITTLE KINDNESSES. On your pastor's birthday, shower him with the zaniest birthday cards you can find. Have all the kids in Sunday school make original birthday cards for the pastor. Take a pastor in town other than your own out to breakfast, but only after you have done that for your pastor. Why not take them both out to breakfast? With no agenda, of course. Buy him a lifetime fishing license. Tell your clothier to call your pastor and tell him he has won a new suit, then pay for the suit, a couple of shirts, and three or four ties after he has gone in to get fitted.

"KIDNAP" THE STAFF. With some fun advance planning, "kidnap" your church staff couples, bring them to a central point, and put them in a bus or large van. (Better yet, pick them up in limousines. Check with funeral directors. They may offer the use of their limos just for the fun of it.) Then give your staff couples a progressive dinner of appreciation at various board members' homes. Make certain you have provided baby-sitting and meals for the kids so that the moms will relax and enjoy. Give large floral bouquets to each of the ladies. Take pictures of each couple and of the whole group and have them framed for each couple as a gift of thanks and remembrance. Videotape the whole thing to catch their surprised faces and show an edited video at the next appropriate church gathering.

3

MARRIAGE AND FAMILY LIFE OF THE PASTOR

Though it is positioned in the middle of the book, I wrote this chapter last to emphasize the importance and complexity of thinking correctly about our pastors' marriages and families.

I was scheduled to have the first draft of this book to NavPress by April 10, 1995. All plans were moving strongly in that direction when God, in His sovereignty, allowed another design to invade the lives of my marriage and family. I know very little about the reasons why we had this invasion, but it did give my family and me the first-hand opportunity to know what it was like to receive tremendous love and care in the middle of a crisis. We have been placed in recent months on another acute learning curve.

In early April 1995, Judy, my wife, and I were planning a car trip to Hot Springs, Arkansas, where I was to consult with the leadership team of a new church. We had looked forward to this trip for weeks. At one level, we needed to "get out of Dodge" and spend some necessary time together without the ringing of phones and the busyness of our lives chasing us. We have often had our best talks while ensconced in a vehicle driving down the road. So, we readily agreed, "Let's take the time and drive."

At another level, I needed to get away from the office and other increasing ministry demands so I could spend uninterrupted time on my lap-top computer working on this book. We agreed that when I was driving we would talk about our lives, discuss issues of interest, listen to tapes, etc. When Judy was driving I would climb into the back seat of our van and tackle this project on the computer. We were even going to take a couple of days on the way home to celebrate our twenty-eighth wedding anniversary in good old Branson, Missouri . . . heehaw!

Judy, not one to complain about much at all, let me know on the trip that she was having a series of headaches that were not going away. In Hot Springs we found ourselves praying in the middle of one night over a very severe headache. In Branson double vision began to plague her. We steamrolled for home. It has never taken longer to drive across Kansas.

By Friday of that week we had the jolting news from a neurologist, after a quick CAT scan, that "there appeared to be an abnormal growth in the area of the pituitary gland." And that was all the information we were left with for an entire weekend, except that Judy's symptoms were getting worse.

I may not be a flaming intellectual, but I do have a semi-wild imagination and a very active mind. That weekend in April our minds and hearts were all over the emotional map. In a most unusual moment, our daughter had even come home from her in-state college with her boyfriend. We shared this news with them and wondered and prayed and cried and planned plans that seemed to go nowhere on such limited information. At moments we were a mess, at other moments we experienced a surge of calm that was startling, and at other moments it was almost life as normal — whatever *normal* means.

I share all this to make an important confession, as a man, as a Christian leader. I found out I am a much better "giver" than "receiver." After all, we are in ministry to give to the needs of others, in particular Christian leaders from around the world, especially pastors. It is our lifework to "give."

One lesson I've learned, and keep learning, is what an arrogant "receiver" I've been, as in I don't need to receive much to get on with what I am called to do. Our gracious, all-knowing God has used this as a deep motive check on how and why I give to others. This has been painful, good, and cleansing for my wife and me as we continue to move with this crisis in our family.

On Tuesday, May 16, 1995, Judy underwent several hours of grueling brain surgery to remove a large tumor from her pituitary gland. Her four days in intensive care were some of the worst for both of our lives. The pathology report came back benign. Praise God! (Would I have written those same two words right there if the report had been cancer? I wonder.) With that report also came the information that parts of the tumor had invaded her sinus cavities, and that further significant treatment would be required because it was the kind of tumor that would grow back.

It is now Saturday, July 29, 1995, and I *must* have this project on my editor's desk Monday at 10:00 A.M., by mutual agreement. Am I a promise keeper, or not? Steve Webb has been extra understanding and forgiving of missed deadlines. The whole NavPress team has extended more grace to me than any new author should ever receive. They have been unusually faithful in lifting us all up in prayer without any hint of "get that book in, or else." They have cared at an incredibly deep level. We have been deeply moved—and encouraged.

Computer literate is one description I would never use for myself, nor would anyone who truly knows me. But in April, when the awful facts began to be known about Judy's tumor, I sent out a number of messages on e-mail seeking prayer. I've never felt so helpless. With regularity, messages came back that were astounding in their to-the-minute timeliness with words of encouragement, concern, and some very necessary admonition for me, in particular, from those who took the time to love us well. Judy's condition was placed on prayer networks around the globe.

We began to receive messages via e-mail and fax from people we didn't even know. One of the most meaningful was also one of the first. It was short, but powerful. It simply read, ". . . on my knees." We wept tears that night that cleansed our fright and pain—we were not alone.

We were in between churches at the time, and a friend's church, not even ours, stepped in to bring meals. Talk about being humbled to the core by some intentional acts of kindness, even those we may take for granted. It was amazing! How that ministered to Judy at a very deep level, knowing that we were eating well. There was always enough for several meals, not just one. It was a demonstration of His grace—there in abundance. Some of our needs were being taken care of in a very deliberate way through the body of Christ.

As this goes to press we are still not out of the woods with regard to Judy's condition. Now that the "crisis of the moment" has passed, people, of necessity, have moved on to praying for the needs and care of other friends. We know we are not forgotten, and with the tremendous demonstrations of love and care we received, we know we can "holler if we need to." And we will, confident that He is there for us through others who have the interest and courage to care.

For now, we wait to see what happens next with Judy's pending treatment. We wait with the assurance that He *is* in charge. And in our waiting we are more profoundly aware, at a more realistic, authentic level, of the importance of giving . . . and receiving.

Why this glimpse at our lives of late? You need to know that when people who care begin to "meddle," even though lovingly, in your life, it is scary and humbling, not a picnic. For most Christian leaders, being vulnerable about their marriage and family lives and all that goes on there is not easy. None of us likes to have his weaknesses exposed. We are much more comfortable with being "well thought of."

Some Christian leaders have a hard, steadfast determination not to let anyone inside. All that has happened to us in these recent months has pulled me up short to show me that I was dangerously close to being one of those kinds of Christian leaders. That was not right on my part.

The loving persistence of a few has taught me valuable new lessons. These moments of pain, helplessness, introspection, and growth have caused me to ponder and wonder about how we can genuinely move toward pastors and other Christian leaders, their marriages, and their families, to encourage them in both times of need and times of relative bliss.

I've even wondered what it would be like to live in a society where everyone knew your every move and made it his "business" to know how much you made and where you went on vacation. Where everyone evaluated you weekly on your "performance" and the kind of relationship you had with your spouse, and gave an opinion on how your kids acted. Where everyone gave conditional approval of how you dressed and how your wife and kids looked, of what kind of car you drove, of how you took care of your home, and of how you spoke to groups. Where everyone expected you to sacrifice your own family priorities for the good of the group and criticized you if you didn't treat him "just so." Where everyone failed to take into account that you also are struggling to have a rich and meaningful family life. Where everyone was suspect that in some parts of your life and relationships all may not be well.

"Oh," you say. "Get off the negative track. Such a negative way of thinking!"

And I say, "Gladly!"

But what you've just read are some of the general, more "benign" things I've heard from clergy, their spouses, and their kids. You should hear the tales that make the rounds — but I won't burden you with the sad details. What is described above is what is happening in too many churches today. Too often it seems to take a crisis of magnitude to get us thinking correctly about the relationships of our pastors, to be sincerely concerned for them and what is happening in their lives.

Even I, who should know better, knew I had picked the wrong time the other evening to call a local pastor friend at 6:15 P.M. One of his kids answered, with the sounds of a meal going on in the background. You see, I was doing this man and his family a "favor" in the future, and I needed to get my schedule settled with them.

My call was good news, my heart was right in desiring to help them, and my intentions were clear.

But my motives were rotten. I had not stopped to consider that this man worked very hard at having the evening meal with his family Monday through Thursday. But I wanted to get this settled so that *I* could get on with *my* evening. At that moment I simply was not functioning with the love, care, and respect I had declared (and still do declare) for this family.

It may not seem like that big of a deal. I wasn't even a part of this man's growing congregation. He had told me to call him anytime at home or office, except between 5:30 and 7:00 P.M., something he had also made clear to his congregation over and over again in a very good way.

I rationalized, "I'm doing this family a favor." What a terrible excuse. Bad judgment. Wrong motives. Selfish justification. What if I wasn't the only one to call?

It doesn't take a rocket scientist to figure this one out. I'd goofed. Deeper than that, I had not stopped to consider the well-being of this pastoral family. I asked the son to have his father call me at his convenience sometime that evening, and got off the phone. When he did return my call he told me that their phone generally rings a dozen or more times during the evening mealtime.

Most of the time this family just takes the phone off the hook so that they are not distracted and can focus on each other. They use the message machine if there is a call they can't miss. To which I said, "Good for you! Don't stop doing that. The likes of me should not interrupt what is of high value to you. I apologize for not thinking about your time with your family."

"C'mon," you say, "you're making a mountain out of a mole-hill. It was only one call, and a good one at that." Consider the following, which I happened to find in an Amish/Mennonite museum in northern Indiana. The author is unknown.

A Fable

The Weight of One Voice

"Tell me the weight of a snowflake,"
a sparrow asked a wild dove.
"Nothing," was the answer.
"In that case I must tell you a marvelous story,"
the sparrow said.
"I sat on the branch of a fir when it began to snow.
Since I didn't have anything better to do,
I counted the snowflakes settling on the twigs and needles
of my branch.
Their number was exactly 3,741,952.
When the next snowflake dropped onto the branch
—weighing nothing, you say—
the branch broke."

Having said that, the sparrow flew off.

The dove thought about the story for a while
and finally said to herself:
"Perhaps
there is only one person's voice
lacking for peace to come about in the world."

Perhaps all your good intentions, or mine, are like that one last snowflake. We need to respect at a deep, deep level the needs of our pastor's marriage and family. We need to trust the strong promptings of the Holy Spirit on when to move in and say or do something, and when to stay away, and yet be there as needed.

So much of life seems to be a balancing act. Which leads me to ask, "Well then, what *can* we do to encourage our pastor's marriage and family life?"

The following suggestions are certainly not exhaustive. In each of the chapters of this book you will find "variations on a theme." You are correct when you notice similar ideas showing up in different contexts. You may want to go through this section with the question in mind, "What would I like to have someone do to encourage my own marriage and family, if I would let them?"

FOR THE PASTORAL MARRIAGE

Showing Appreciation and Affirmation

Would you allow me to get on a bit of a soapbox? In my opinion, and a host of others' opinions as well, the pastoral spouse is one of the most forgotten, faithful people within the church today. I am amazed and appalled at how bypassed she is.

So many congregations simply figure that if the pastor's wife is really sharp, talented at teaching, and can play the piano or sing, then, hey, have we got a good deal, or what? I think this two-for-the-price-of-one mentality is an obnoxious odor in God's nostrils. It is certainly a serious affront to the value and worth of these women who are dedicating their lives to His service as wonderfully created and unique partners in ministry.

I say it is high time we made right what has been wrong for so many years. Would you be willing to join me in an all-out "conspiracy of love"? We need to make some extraordinary efforts at affirming and encouraging our pastors' wives. Ready . . . set . . . let's go!

MAKE A BIG DEAL OVER THIS LADY'S BIRTHDAY. And don't forget the birthdays of the wives of your other staff members. How about a PSBC Committee (Pastoral Spouse Birthday Club Committee) for your church? Someone out there in your congregation would be dynamite for this ministry of encouragement. Is that someone you?

Send your pastoral couples off for a night or two at a bed and breakfast on *her* birthday . . . such a deal!

If your pastor's wife's birthday is in the spring, do a garden shower for her, as in coordinating a bunch of bedding plants to beautify their home and then having volunteers show up to prepare the soil and plant the flowers where *she* would like them planted.

This idea came from a lifelong friend Judy and I thank God for. She also happens to be a tremendous pastor's wife. On a visit to their home some weeks ago she told me that in her part of the world flower gardens are a big deal, and she was not born with a green thumb. She would like to learn from some of the women in their church who have beautiful yards, but with kids in college they do not have the extra funds for such luxuries. She was not complaining—that is not her nature—just being wistful and honest. With her usual sparkle in her eyes she said, "I think a flower shower would be one of the most encouraging happenings in my life right now." I'm confident your pastor's wife would like that too.

GIVE THE GIFT OF A SPOTLESSLY CLEAN HOUSE. Give your pastor's wife a gift certificate from a home-cleaning service in your community. It is a little easier for approved strangers to come into your home to clean than to be invaded by members of the congregation—unless y'all know each other *real well*. Make sure this is the super-duper, top-to-bottom, deep-cleaning package, and not just a polite swipe at the floors.

The above idea would be especially helpful if your pastor's spouse must work, if they have small children, if an illness has messed up the family schedule, if you know visitors are coming to the pastor's home, or if you simply want to do something nice for that dear woman just because it's Thursday and you love her—and for no reason other than that.

SHE'S NOT AN ANSWERING MACHINE. Don't treat your pastor's wife like she is the church secretary and knows all about what is happening at the church—unless she *is* the church secretary. This lady is not a message machine for her husband. If she should forget your message, both you and her husband would be displeased. Call the office during office hours to leave a message for the pastor.

ALLOW PRIVACY IN HER PERSONAL LIFE. "Many things your family considers personal are public knowledge for her family. The church doesn't need to know when they're planning to have babies, or all the details of their vacation, or how much their new couch cost. Some pastors' wives feel as if they are constantly giving an account for every purchase. If she wears a great new outfit, compliments are appropriate. Questions about where she bought it aren't" (Linda Riley, *Esteem Them Highly*).

Also, allow your pastor's wife her style, even if it's not yours. Don't talk about the difference to someone else. Let her be her, and you be you.

PROVIDE RECIPES. If your pastoral couple is extra busy, pass along some of your "quick and easy-to-fix" dinner recipes for people on the move.

GET THE MASSAGE. Here in Denver there is a wonderful Christian woman who is a massage therapist. She considers part of her work/ministry giving Christian leaders and their spouses massages. Ahhh. . . . Find such a person in your community and give that pastoral couple such a luxury treatment on their anniversary, or birthdays, or if the kids have been sick, or it's Friday morning and it just seems right.

WATCH YOUR INTRODUCTIONS. When introducing your pastoral couples to friends, do not say, "This is our pastor's wife" or "This is our pastor, Matt Heard, and his wife, Arlene." Introduce her by her own name before informing your friends about her husband.

Do say, "I'd like for you to meet one of the pastoral couples in our church. This is Matt and Arlene Heard." Think about it. Arlene *does* have a last name, but so often we introduce men with a last name and leave the lady dangling. Not good—or correct. Arlene is not an appendage to Matt. She is a valued person all by herself. And fortunately, she happens to be deeply grateful that she is married to Matt. You could even add, "Arlene is one of the most wonderful women you could ever meet, and Matt just happens to be our senior pastor at Sunshine Community Church in Grand Rapids." Since Matt and Arlene are personal friends, an extraordinary couple, good parents, and strongly committed to their ministry roles, I can pick on them just a little.

Learn to introduce people with a first and last name, and briefly tell what it is you value about them as persons, not just about the roles they play out day to day. That can be a second line of introduction. For example, "I'd like for you to meet my good friends, Matt and Arlene Heard. Arlene is one of those people who has a compelling consistency about her that comes from her deep, caring heart for others. Matt is a man of deep and lively convictions. Arlene is an excellent model of what a pastor's wife should be, and Matt is one of the most stimulating and challenging senior pastors you could know."

In short, we need to honor, affirm, and encourage people even in how we introduce them. Let's have a practice session. How will you introduce that lady who also happens to be your pastor's spouse?

TEACH HER MORE ABOUT ENTERTAINING. If you are one of those alive, fun, older-in-years-but-not-older-in-attitude women in your church who has the gift of hospitality; if you know how to make people feel comfortable in your home and can cook up a storm—or at least know where the best deli is in town; if you can set a beautiful table with all the right linens, dishes, glasses, and tableware—and not necessarily with the finest of china and crystal; if you are creative and can throw a great party for from 4 to 104 people at a "moment's notice"; then you, my friend, are a candidate for this next suggestion (and I want to be invited to your home the next time I'm in town!).

In our transient, fast-paced lives, since we no longer live close to moms and aunts and grandmothers and older sisters who in past generations passed on "homemaking" skills, I find many wonderful young women who are glad to be in ministry with their husbands but who are "frightened" about entertaining simply, economically, and even elegantly, if the occasion calls for it, because the mentoring opportunities have not been there for them.

Well, if you are one of those ladies who does know what to do, I have a fun challenge for you. How about if you begin a Great Hostesses Entertainment Forum? Or a New Brides Cooking School? Or Warm Welcomes and Parties for All Occasions 101? Invite the young pastors' wives and female staff members and their friends who are also young wives (a group of up to ten works well) to your home once a quarter, or to the home of someone you know with a large kitchen. Tell them you are all going to work together all day to throw a party for yourselves and your husbands that night. Set a theme for the food ahead of time so that they can begin to think about what they will be doing. Then, beginning with a light brunch, help them think through decor to enhance the party; hand out recipes; go shopping together for the goods; return to prepare the food and fun; and then you and your husband, or others from the congregation, can come in and serve the couples and do the cleanup. You would be doing a significant service in the development of these young women—modeling so much for them—if you would accept this challenge. And let them know you are available for questions anytime. They'll be back!

DO A FOOD SHOWER. How about an annual food shower, from a list of their choosing—and not just at Christmas?

BE A TEMPORARY CATERER. Offer to bring in a complete meal when you know your pastoral family is entertaining guests in their home for several days.

BE A HIRED HAND. Call your pastor's spouse and offer to give her a full day of your time to do whatever she wants. You do the cleaning, painting, cooking, baby-sitting—whatever.

BE CONSIDERATE OF HOUSING. Churches should understand that housing is a huge factor in the spouse's contentment level. The home is more than a place to live, it is a nest and a place of security and comfort. If the wife dislikes her home, its location, its state of disrepair, or whatever, no one in that family is going to be ministering contentedly.

There are fewer parsonages today than in previous years. I think it a good idea, financially, for the pastor to build equity in a home of his choosing. However, should you be one of those congregations that still graciously provides a home for your pastors, do all you can in between pastors to make the home what the incoming family would like. Allow the new pastor's wife to choose colors, wallpaper, and carpet according to the needs and tastes of the family. Don't skimp on this!

One young couple I knew were very excited when they were told they were moving into a new parsonage, and that it would be ready for them as soon as they arrived. What they should have been told is that the church had not previously owned this building: it had broken windows, the toilets would not flush, the carpeting carried the stains and odor from dogs that had not made it all the way outside, and the house had sat idle for so long that they could sweep up a quart of mice "poop" from the kitchen cupboards to sprinkle on their flowers in the spring. I'm not making this one up! Things of this type happen all too frequently where congregations do not place a solid value on honoring and affirming pastoral couples in all the dimensions of their lives.

The couple that was invited to live in these deplorable conditions rented a motel room for a week at their own expense, worked fourteen-hour days to make the place livable, and have been there eleven years now because they knew they were called of God to that community. Just last year someone apologized to them for not having a better place for them to live when they first arrived. Amazing! Best of all, our Lord has rewarded this couple's faithfulness, and a church is growing, at last, in a small town in mid-America where pastors used to last only for three to five years.

CREATE A CARING PASTORAL ENVIRONMENT. If I were ever "forced" to make a "Top Ten List of Pastors' Wives," the lady who wrote these words would probably be on that list: "I think senior pastors need to spend personal time with their staff and spouses for fun, fellowship, and sometimes sort of a 'checkup' on how things are going. Staff spouses need to have an opportunity to express needs, grievances, ask questions, etc. If they can't have regular meetings with the senior or administrative pastor or board, then communication usually becomes more subversive and unhealthy. Often, the staff wife has no one to talk to, or can only talk to the senior pastor's wife, which can put the senior wife in a difficult position when there are misunderstandings or unmet needs. There needs to be some legitimate avenue for both the staff person and the spouse to express their frustrations and share their challenges in a confidential and caring setting" (Linda Riley, *Esteem Them Highly*).

Would you be willing to make certain that such an environment is available in your church? Offer to your church board to help this happen.

IN CASE OF MORAL FAILURE. If moral failure happens on the part of the pastor, make certain the wife and children have safe and qualified counseling for as long as they need it. Make sure for the pastor, too, of course, but too often the family is forgotten in this kind of crisis.

INCLUDE THE SPOUSE. Spouses should always be invited to attend conferences pastors choose to participate in, where appropriate, with the church bearing all the costs. Put that in as a part of your church budget, and let pastoral couples know this at the time you call them to your church.

TAKE A SPOUSE TO LUNCH. One pastor's wife told me that after five years at a new pastorate at a fair-sized church, she had yet to be invited out to lunch or to do anything special, just for fun "girl things." That's unbelievable! And a crime. Don't assume that the wives of your pastors have a full social calendar. They have numerous events in their home, but hardly any in other homes.

FOR MEN ONLY. If you have already established a relationship with your pastor, talk to him about giving his first and best attention to his wife. Tell him you know about the challenges of marriage personally and that you will be praying for him. You could tell him about how you came to realize the importance of honoring your wife in the ways you needed to, and she needs for you to. In general, notice when your pastor demonstrates love for his wife, let him know you noticed, and cheer him on.

Gary Smalley and John Trent have some of the best words on honoring one another that I know of. I thank them for the following word picture: a man should consider whether his wife feels like an everyday dinner plate or whether she feels honored, cherished, and secure—like a fine china plate. Both spouses and fine china are special, both increase in value, both are hard to replace, both may require time to fix, and neither can be purchased in a discount store. Good china, like a good spouse, never loses its quality, and we are hurt when it is broken or cracked. You could tell the pastor about this word picture and then give him a fine china teacup and saucer to give his wife. Tell him the gift is to be from him because she is special to him.

THANK THE WIVES PUBLICLY. Take out an ad in your town newspaper to thank your staff wives for their support and dedication. Include pictures.

KIDNAP THE WIFE. Some night when you know your pastor will be home (so he can take care of the kids), swoop in and kidnap his wife for a fun "lady's night out." Surprise!

Time Together

DEAL WITH THE INDIVIDUAL. If the pastor or his spouse offends you, deal directly with the individual. *Never* complain about the husband to the wife, or about the wife to the husband.

THE NUMBER-ONE PRIORITY. Encourage your pastors to make time with their spouses their number-one priority of all their human relationships, and let them know you think it is the top priority.

ENCOURAGE PASTORAL DATING. Be bold enough to ask, in a loving way, when your pastor last went on a date with his wife to a place she wanted to go. To the degree that your prior relationship justifies it, hold him accountable, and let the wife know you are holding him accountable. She will delight in knowing someone is in her court.

GIVE THEM TIME OFF. Once a quarter, or at the very least twice a year, allow your pastoral couples a weekend off, just like "regular folk." Hold the pastoral marriage in high enough esteem that their free nights and weekends are kept intact, even if something comes up at church. *Nothing* is more important.

PLAN A UNIQUE DINNER PARTY. There resides a couple in Indiana of which I wish there were ten in every congregation. They invite the pastor and his family over to their home for dinner. When they arrive, the pastoral couple is invited to sit in the living room, just the two of them, to visit and get caught up with each other. The host couple takes the kids into the kitchen and explains that on this night "we are all going to play restaurant," as in taking orders for the food, serving it, etc., if the kids are old enough.

The dining room table is set for two. Or perhaps you want to set a small table in the corner of the living room, with soft lights, candles, and romantic music. While one of the hosts serves the pastoral couple tasty appetizers, the other feeds the kids early, and gives them instructions on how to serve their parents. Then one of the kids rings the dinner bell and announces dinner.

These fortunate pastoral couples are always surprised that they are dining alone. "Oh, how nice," says Kim. "Scott, what do we do with all this time alone together? What shall we talk about? Are Ben and Elizabeth okay?"

To which Scott thinks, *Oh, how awkward*, and then replies, "Well, honey, I hope they are okay. Sounds like they are having a good time without us. What's going on here? This is spooky . . . just you and me. When was the last time it was just us? I thought we were coming over here to get acquainted with these people. We could have talked at home after the kids went to bed. We've been tricked!"

To be fair to some good friends whose names are mentioned above, this is not what we would find "our" Scott and Kim saying. Scott would be trying to figure out how to come over again next week, and the evening would be thoroughly delightful, a time of real refreshment.

My Indiana friends keep the kids occupied for the whole meal, making certain the couple has everything they need, just like in a fancy restaurant—time, quiet, good food, great dessert, and more time just to talk in the living room. Then as the evening draws to a close they might come in and spend some moments with the couple and pray for each member of the family.

VARIATIONS ON A THEME. This is one idea on which I can imagine several great variations.

Invite the couple over and have the food all ready to go, with the firm understanding that no dishes are to be done by the pastoral couple, then disappear with their kids (if you know them well enough) and leave the couple alone in your home with the music, the food, the lights low, and the phone off the hook—a total environment for just them. If you have a hot tub, ask them to bring their swimsuits. Have a bundle of fresh towels ready for them, and let them know the hour you plan to return. They'll figure out the rest. A mini-retreat for four hours. Wow!

Another variation: When the couple arrive with their kids, have another couple from the church (make certain the kids and the pastoral couple already know them) waiting to whisk the kids away to their place for the whole night. Then do the dinner thing very slowly, waiting on them in elegant style, staying out of their way so they can talk, talk, talk, and then sending them home with loving, firm instructions to take the phone off the hook and sleep in minus the kids. Tell them to call you when they do wake up, because you will be bringing them breakfast in bed—before the kids get home. Are we having fun yet?

Some of this could get to be such great fun that you'll want to spread the joy around. How about getting several other couples in your church to go in with you to make your primary ministry ministering to the staff, their spouses, and their kids? Go wild, get crazy, as well as simple, profound, and meaningful, and keep your church staff off guard. By that I mean never, or at least hardly ever, let the staff know when the next moment of love and care may be coming their way. You've got creative friends there in your church—go for it! And let me know the end results of your grand conspiracy.

GIVE YOUR PASTORAL COUPLE A COUPON GOOD FOR COFFEE AND MUFFINS AT A COFFEE BAR OR PASTRY SHOP. Tell them there will be a table waiting for them at a certain hour on a certain day (after you've made arrangements with the store owner). Then leave a gift of appreciation for them before they arrive. Tell the store owner what you are up to—who these people are, that you love 'em to pieces, and to make certain they have the best service. You'll be ministering to the store owner as much as the couple.

ENSURE THE PASTORAL COUPLE'S PRIVACY. One of the hazards of church ministry is that members know too much about the personal lives of the pastors. So make certain that the staff members' days off are known and respected throughout the congregation. Make it a habit to leave them alone for these vitally important times. As you pick up the phone, remember that any night could be their date night.

LIMIT THE NUMBER OF EVENINGS PER WEEK A PASTOR WILL BE ON DUTY.

INVITE A CHRISTIAN PSYCHOLOGIST IN TO TEACH BOTH THE STAFF AND THE CONGREGATION ABOUT BOUNDARIES.

BABY-SIT THE PASTOR'S KIDS. Make it your aim to sit once a month with the pastor's kids so that the couple can be free to do whatever they want. Set up the time from month to month.

IF THE PASTORAL COUPLE REALISTICALLY DOESN'T HAVE THE FUNDS TO GO OUT, GET THEM SOME MONEY.

Enriching Pastoral Marriages
In chapter 6 you will find some good options for enriching pastoral marriages. Consider especially Gray Fox Ranch, the Lake Martin Marriage Retreat, Paraklesis Ministries, Restoration Ministries, and Life Enrichment's four-day marriage assessment. They have excellent programs for clergy couples who want and need to enrich their marriages. All offer week-long programs that will strengthen and change individuals and couples' lives.

HELP ENRICH YOUR PASTORAL MARRIAGE. Send each of your pastoral couples to the Family Life Conference. Pay all their expenses. For more information call 800/333-1703. Or refer to countless options in chapter 6.

START A PRAYER NETWORK. How about having a prayer network in your church that prays specifically for each person on staff, each pastoral spouse, and each pastoral kid? Get ready to watch God at work.

ENCOURAGE YOUR STAFF TO GO WITH THEIR SPOUSES TO PLACES OF LEARNING AND GROWING TOGETHER. Do all you can to help make certain the church funds this, in the knowledge that it is for the couple, and ultimately the whole church.

ANOTHER VERY IMPORTANT ITEM. Don't "force" your pastoral couples to go somewhere if they sincerely do not want to. Find out what would help build their marriage from their perspective and help make it happen.

Family Matters

INCLUDE THE KIDS. One pastor said, "Invite us over with our children. Many don't seem to want to do this. We love it when they do, because we think our kids are great. People who make our kids feel loved and special also make us feel loved and special."

REMEMBER THE KIDS' BIRTHDAYS. Don't go overboard on this tip—in other words, don't spoil them—but make sure you know the birthdays of all the staff's children and send them a card to let them know that you know who they are and that you thank God for them personally, not just because they are their parents' children. At other times let those kids know the good impact their parents have on you.

RESPECT THE KIDS' INDIVIDUALITY. Kids can see through hidden agendas faster than we adults can. Therefore, value them for who they are, not whose they are. Children are sensitive to being used. They don't appreciate being made much of in order to gain favor with their parents. They know when others are fishing for information; therefore, refrain from asking questions about their parents' actions, feelings, or opinions. If you need to know that bad, ask their mom or dad.

Also, don't expect the pastor's kids to be perfect. Yours aren't. Show them understanding and care. Realize that pastors' kids are just kids. Some are shy, some are loud, some are hyper, some are full of the dickens—just like other people's kids. Give them room to be themselves. If these kids should do something a little off, or even shocking, don't say, ". . . and you're the pastor's son/daughter?!" Those, or anything close to them, are not helpful words.

DON'T REQUIRE YOUR PASTOR, HIS SPOUSE, OR HIS CHILDREN TO FIT INTO A MOLD. Let each of them be uniquely who he or she is.

BUILD UP THE PARENTS TO THE KIDS. One of the most fun things I do with older kids, and even with little tykes, is to tell them what terrific parents they have. For example, "Brandon, you have two of the best parents any kids could have. They are some of the best people I know. How did you get them to be your parents? That's amazing! I love your mom and dad a bunch!" Of course, the kids will look at you weird, but I can guarantee that something good and special is happening if such an honest encounter can be well-timed every few months.

Just this morning in church (this is obviously a Sunday afternoon) I told the pastor's teenage daughter, "Your dad preached a powerful message today. It hit me right where I needed to be hit. And your mom sang a beautiful, meaningful song. I sure am thankful for your parents and all they do here." The daughter beamed, the mom blushed slightly, and the dad asked me to repeat my words (ha!). I want those kids to know that what their parents are doing in ministry is paying off in some important ways.

A REMINDER. ONE MORE TIME: RESPECT THE PASTOR'S PRIVATE TIME WITH THE FAMILY.

GIVE THE PASTOR TIME TO BE WITH HIS KIDS. As best you can, make certain the pastor has the opportunity get to his kids' sports games, school plays, etc., and that he has time off to play with them. Attendance at sporting events, plays, musicals, concerts, etc., should come before church activities such as midweek services and socials. Work hard in your church to create a climate wherein the children will not hate the pastorate because the pastor has time for everyone else and not for them.

A young pastor once called me on a Saturday perplexed. His son's soccer team had made it all the way to the area championships. The game was scheduled for Sunday at 10:30 A.M., and he wanted to be there in the worst way. What should he do? Some people would disagree, but to me that was a no-brainer. So the pastor called all his elders and told them what was up, and that he had a speaker and music all lined up for Sunday morning. He had even tape-recorded an introduction for the speaker to tell his congregation why he was not there. He didn't get fired, and his son thought he was awesome and that the church leaders were too. One family did leave the church, but they needed to leave anyway. God was honored, and probably enjoyed the soccer game with those little munchkins He had created running all over the field so full of life.

PROVIDE AN ADEQUATE SALARY. Allow the pastor's family to do what the average family in your church is able to do.

GIVE THE PASTOR FREE TICKETS. One pastor told me, "The only time we can go to football, baseball, or basketball games as a family is when gracious people give us tickets. It's a real treat. We love it." Give up an occasional game of your own season tickets and do something different with your own spouse. For both families there can be real benefit.

SURPRISE THE PASTOR WITH AN AFTERNOON OFF. Arrange with your pastor's secretary to give him a Friday afternoon free. Letting her in on the secret will ensure that no one with a genuine need is turned away. She can schedule a long appointment in your name, then you can call at 3:00 P.M. and say, "Pastor, you have ten minutes to pack up and get out of there. The rest of the day is for you. Go home to your family!"

FACILITATE THE PASTOR'S VACATIONS. One pastor made these comments about vacation times: "We have had many special family vacations that we otherwise could not have afforded, in donated trailers, condos, and cabins. These were wonderful gifts that we have never sought, but have simply had them offered to us. At this current church one family has assured us that we can have one week every summer at their lake cottage to be alone with our family. What memories we are making up there at that lake year after year."

One group of seven couples has vacationed together annually for years. They have simply made it a point of taking one of their pastoral families each year, no matter where they go.

Often a nice, relaxing vacation at a quality resort is financially out of reach for pastors. Suggest that your pastor and his family join your family for vacation and let them know you want to pay a percentage of all their expenses (consider 50 percent). This allows them to keep their dignity intact and enjoy a wonderful vacation for the price of a mediocre one. You need to make certain that the families are compatible.

This last one may get me in trouble with the relatives, but a visit with most relatives is just that—a visit with the relatives. It's not a vacation, a time to let down and relax. However, many pastoral families cannot afford to do anything else. Help them make a real vacation happen apart from the relatives every once in a while.

TAKE CARE OF THE PASTORAL COUPLE'S KIDS AFTER CHURCH. That way they can talk to other people. One single woman regularly gets the pastor's toddler from the nursery between services and after church to allow the pastor's wife time to talk with visitors and friends.

GIVE CREATIVE COUPONS. Give the pastoral couple a coupon that reads, "Four-course dinner delivered to your door at 6:00 P.M. on the night of your choice—with three days notice." Or "Baby-sitting provided for the weekend you want to get away on a romantic encounter." Use your imagination. What other coupons could you write for your pastoral couple?

SHOW INTEREST IN THE PASTORAL VOCATION. A pastor told me this recently: "Last week two couples in our small group had the sensitivity to simply ask us what it's like to be a pastoral family. They asked detailed questions like, 'What is it that you wouldn't expect laypeople to be able to understand about the pastorate?' It was a really odd experience to have them show so much interest. It was also very affirming."

A GRAB BAG OF TIPS FOR SUPPORTING YOUR PASTOR'S FAMILY.

- ▶ If you have "tons" of frequent flyer miles, let the pastor and his family go somewhere on them.
- ▶ Provide a family membership at the local health club or Y.
- ▶ Buy them an answering machine and encourage them to use it, especially during meal times. Let them know you are going to test them and see if it is on.
- ▶ Arrange for a day out for the whole family, including a picnic just for them.
- ▶ Give each of the staff kids a coupon book to McDonald's.
- ▶ If you are at the age when you could be a grandparent, or are one, be surrogate grandparents to the pastor's kids. We all need to stay connected intergenerationally.
- ▶ During the Christmas program, video specifically the staff kids and give the parents the cassette.
- ▶ Take your pastor and spouse out to dinner and *don't* talk about church at all. That will be a test of discipline, and it will be good for each of you!
- ▶ Leave cinnamon rolls on the pastor's front porch (with a note telling who they are from). Make sure they're out of the way of animals.
- ▶ Invite the couple to a murder mystery dinner. These are a barrel of fun, especially if you get into costume and really play the parts.
- ▶ Invite the couple to take ballroom dance classes with you. You pay. Then for graduation get all dressed up and dance up a storm.
- ▶ If you live in a city with historic districts, take a walking tour with the pastoral couple and have a meal at a sidewalk cafe.
- ▶ Consider taking the pastor's kids Christmas shopping so the kids can buy "real presents" for their parents.

CHAPTER

4

MINISTRY LIFE
OF THE PASTOR

W hen I was a "squirrelly, smelly, naive, overzealous" youth
pastor in a Baptist church in Southern California in the
late 1960s, in the middle of the "Jesus movement," the
church in which I had the privilege to serve had a Christian school.
My office was located off a busy hallway (truth be known, my
office was too raucous to exist in the regular office area). The third-
grade classroom of the school was at one end of the hall, my office
at the other. During one of those years, the music minister (who
also happened to be the principal of the school) had a daughter in
the third grade. Her desk was positioned where she could look out
the door, up the hall, and keep a persistent view of my office, where
things were seldom "normal." In fact, I used to wave at Joyce, a
bright third-grade social wizard who did not miss anything, almost
every time I would come or go from my office. This often got her
(and me) in "trouble" with her terrific teacher. It also provided for
a lively relationship with a delightful young girl who was one of
the best spontaneous gigglers I've ever known.

On one of those rare mornings when I was in the church early,
Joyce's mom was waiting for me at my office, having just seen me
drive into the church parking lot. Evelyn, the mom, was trying to
look serious, but her eyes were twinkling. "I thought you should
know that Joyce asked a big question about you today. She knows
what her dad does here at the church and school. She thinks she
knows what the other ministers do because of what she sees them
do on Sundays. But on our way to school this morning she asked me,
'Is Wes's job just talking on the telephone, laughing a lot, and listening to loud music until Mrs. Stewart [the third-grade teacher]
tells him to turn it down?'"

Good question, Joyce. What does any kind of pastor do with
all his time? Thankfully, this mom of hers was more tickled than
perplexed because she was a woman who understood the pressures
and variables of ministry, since she was a wonderful, giving, committed spouse in a church staff family.

Our staff at that church had a good and growing relationship. (It
wasn't always great. But to sum up my years there, I look back on that
time with fond memories.) No one on staff was a slouch in the "time-

put-in" category. We learned to trust each other, and gratefully, the church board also trusted us. Therefore, each of us on staff gave well to what we were individually and collectively called to do.

But I have been in a number of congregations in this world of ours where people really do wonder what the pastor does with all the allotted time. In some places that wondering is justified. In other places people do not know all that a pastor does. After all, Sunday services and midweek programs aren't all that long. And if a pastor has any staff at all—what *does* he do with all his time?

The myth out there is that most pastors golf on Mondays; have staff meetings for an hour or two on Tuesdays, after which they go to lunch with one of the elders or deacons; coach their kid's Little League team on Wednesdays; conduct funerals on Thursdays; fold bulletins and drink coffee on Fridays with the senior citizens; officiate weddings on Saturdays; and hey, we're back to Sunday again.

Pierce Harris, a Methodist minister, was quoted by Marshall Shelley in *Christianity Today* as saying,

> The modern preacher has to
> > make as many visits as a country doctor,
> > shake as many hands as a politician,
> > prepare as many briefs as a lawyer,
> > and see as many people as a specialist.
> He has to be
> > as good an executive as the president of a university,
> > as good a financier as a bank president,
> and in the midst of it all,
> > he has to be so good a diplomat
> > that he could umpire a baseball game
> > between the Knights of Columbus
> > and the Ku Klux Klan.

The Alban Institute in Washington, D.C., did an excellent major study on ministry stress. Here, briefly, is the outline of that report on "The Seven Major Stressors in Ministry," each point followed with my personal editorial comments. What are some of those stressors?

EXPECTATIONS AND PROJECTIONS

Being Compared with Past Pastors
or Other Pastors One Has Known

We all know the grass is supposedly greener on the other side of the fence, unless you are pastored by someone on *my* "Ten Best Pastors in the World" list. Frankly, when we begin to compare two different people, one is always going to come up in second place. We need to think through our motivation for making this kind of comparison. What do we want to prove by making this comparison? Will it be for the benefit of the pastor about whom we may have some concern? Will the comparison build up or put down? What's in it for us personally? Read Ephesians 4:29 in the *New International Version* and then proceed with what is best.

Dealing with the Different Traditions Represented
in Today's Churches

Reconciliation is beginning to happen between many denominations and ethnic groups. Many, especially nondenominational churches, seem to be moving toward being "LuCharisEpiscoMethoBapTerian assemblies," which isn't all bad as long as we understand our biblical distinctives and stop fussing about our nonessential differences. We can all learn to put less emphasis on the unimportant things and leave time for those with real significance.

Wanting the Pastor to Be the Resident "Holy Man"

Pastors *should* know better than to do the negative, sinful things they do in life, but *so should we all* who claim Jesus Christ as Lord of our lives. God didn't say "Be holy" only to the clergy. His Son simply but profoundly said once, "He that is without sin among you, let him first cast a stone." And one of the greatest pastors of all time once wrote, "Confess your sins to one another." Whew! It's risky business, living in Christian community with one another. But we *really are* in this thing called *life* together.

The Pastoral Family *Must* Live the Model Christian Life

Absolutely! What do they think we are paying them "big bucks" for anyway! They must be an example and keep up the "ideal" of what the model Christian life is. How dare they let their kids run all over the church! By the way, where are mine? Enough said.

Uncertainty on How to Measure a Pastor's Success

We all think we know, if we're honest with ourselves. But how do you measure a pastor's success? Way down deep I don't think it has much to do with people numbers or money numbers or even years of service in the Lord's army. Every pastor and congregation must carefully ponder this question individually. What are God's standards for *your own* success before Him?

ROLE CONFUSION

Lack of Clarity About the Position
Gives Everyone an Opinion

Most "job descriptions" in any ministry today are not clear. They're too lofty, too ideal. When I got to be a "regular person" in the pew and not on a church staff a few years ago, I was invited to be on the pastoral search committee for our church. We asked the congregation to give us their ideas on what they wanted in a senior pastor. It was my role (a clear one, I might add) to take those responses and put them into a document for the committee. Well, I couldn't help it, but I concluded the report with the following, ". . . and able to leap tall buildings in a single bound like Superman, walk on water or perform other miracles like Jesus, preach like Chuck Swindoll, counsel like Larry Crabb, focus on every family in the church like Jim Dobson, cook all the church dinners like Graham Kerr, play ball at the men's outings like Michael Jordan, John Elway, or Jose Canseco, and sing like Larnelle Harris or Steve Green . . . all at the same time!" The consulting side of our ministry does have some excellent thoughts on job descriptions should you, as a leader in your own church, be truly interested in your pastor functioning with clarity, focus, and simplicity.

WORK OVERLOAD

The Job Is Never Done

That's true—this side of eternity. Each occupation and calling has both joys and trials, but what if you had to prepare a message weekly to bring everyone you work with (or for) closer to God? How would you handle that pressure? And people are always having babies, dying, getting married, and having personal and family crises with no particular schedule in mind.

A book every pastor and caring parishioner needs to read is *The Contemplative Pastor* by Eugene Peterson. The chapter on "The Unbusy Pastor" alone is worth the price of the book. He writes, "If I'm not busy making my mark in the world or doing what everyone expects me to do, what do I do? What is my proper work? What does it mean to be a pastor? If no one asked me to do anything, what would I do?"

"Three things," Dr. Peterson says. "I can be a pastor who prays." "I can be a pastor who preaches." "I can be a pastor who listens."

In between those sentences, Dr. Peterson masterfully defines the basic and fulfilling role of pastor. I've watched numerous pastors read this chapter and with red-rimmed eyes and huge sighs say, "I fully believe what Peterson is describing. I believe he is defining the biblical perspective of pastoring. How I wish that could be me, but if that is what I did in my church I wouldn't have a job. So much more is expected of me." That is worth some pondering, from both sides of the pulpit. We all need to think through "what is wrong with this picture?"

Needs of the People Always Outstrip Time and Energy

That is also true, this side of eternity. In an increasingly dysfunctional world the stress and pressures all of us are facing continue to increase year by year. It is relatively normal to hope that we can call up our pastor, or at least *a* pastor, and get some of the wise counsel we need from time to time. And our pastors want to be able to give us their time. But, when is it important to ask—or not to ask? How or when do pastors say "not right now" or even "no"? This is a hard decision—very hard—for pastors who are true shepherds who sincerely love their flocks.

CONFLICT

Trying to Be the Bridge Between Conflicting Groups in the Church

Oh, boy! All members want the pastor to be on "their" side. Talk about needing the wisdom of Solomon! Uniquely, the Bible states that we are all supposed to be ministers of reconciliation. So when there is known conflict in a local fellowship we all need to participate in the reconciling and not just leave it all up to the pastor. Pastors can stretch only so far between two opposing groups before they break.

What If Staff Isn't Working Out—Or a Board Member, or the Pastor?

This is tough. We all hope people will work out when they enter a new position, paid or volunteer. Too often both sides do not fully understand what is required of the position. Too often we seek employees/ministry staff without regard to the overall master plan for the church. Too often in our churches we know people who are winsome, charming, full of life, and we think they can fill any ministry position because they simply love people. Not so. That is not how you would hire people in your business.

We are all quick to evaluate our pastors. But I have yet to be in a church that evaluates how well the board is "boarding" individually or as a group. How do we rate the success or failure of this great group of volunteers? How do we nurture our volunteer staff as well as those on salary?

And what do we do if a pastor is simply not making it? Even as I write this, some very good friends in another state are agonizing over what to do with a fundamentally good man who is in a very misplaced pastoral position. There are no easy answers here. But the ideas that follow will hopefully help you move with strength and courage in these less "fun," more difficult areas.

Many Expect the Pastor to Have All the Answers

About what? Just because a pastor knows a little Greek and a little Hebrew, has been to Bible school and/or seminary, and sounds like he can speak on any topic, he can't, even though some pastors may give that impression. Even though he is a loving shepherd who is supposed to listen well to the heart, we somehow expect our pastors to have the advice we need on any given issue of life. Too often we want to be told what to do, think, and feel instead of being encouraged to ponder life's confusion for ourselves or in the community of caring friends. After all, if we ask the pastor what to do and he's wrong, then we are off the hook and he is not a very good pastor. That's not fair to either you or him.

JOB INSECURITY

Salary Dependent on Approval

The pastor's economic well-being and vocational position almost totally depend on the approval and goodwill of the congregation. Yowee! Can you imagine a job where everything depends on if the majority likes you? Pastors who preach with any kind of a prophetic voice are in danger here. If the pastor is not giving "them" what "they" like, the pastor could be history. This seems to be even more true in independent churches where the pastor has no denominational structure or adjudicatory in which to find care and safety. We would all truly like to believe that politics are not "that much" of a concern in most congregations, but congregations are made up of people with opinions. What we do with those opinions can make or break a pastor, and a whole church.

KEY CAREER POINTS

First Pastorate or a First Position Within a Large Church

I've heard it said by knowledgeable heads of church groups that the roughest times in a pastor's ministry are the first five years or years fifteen to twenty-five. What makes that so, I'm not certain. I have seen many fine young pastors come out of their schools so determined to make a go of "church." But unless there is the opportunity of some good mentoring (which there rarely is), the beginnings of a ministry can be extra stressful. Moving to a much larger, new, significant position can have the same effect. All of us will live with different measures of tension when we are placed into new situations outside our comfort zones. A liberal extension of grace is always a wonderful gift to give and receive at these points in time.

Changing Ministries or Positions Within an Established Ministry

Again, change attacks our comfort zones. It is necessary for everyone involved to retool working relationships and expectations and make them realistic. We can never err when we extend extra grace in situations like this.

Long Pastorates

The stress level here is uniquely in two directions. First, there is the pastor who is retiring. One evening in our family room some friends were gathered from around the country. A recently retired pastor was one of our guests. In the middle of an intense discussion about relationships in organizations and churches this dear man blurted out, "You have no idea what it's like to be a pastor for forty-five years and then be put out to pasture with nothing to do." He was desperately trying to find a new place of service. But his particular church group even insisted that he move at least two hundred miles away from the church and town where he had served for years. Talk about the pain of isolation and loneliness, and the insecurity of starting all over at age seventy-one. In my opinion, this was not right for him and his wife.

Second, more often than I care to admit, a strange phenomenon happens in churches where there has been a long pastorate. Over and over again I've heard about pastors not surviving for very many years if they follow someone who has been the senior pastor at a church for a long, long time, or the founding pastor, or any pastor with some measure of strength or charisma. Among many who minister to pastors, this is called the "Sacrificial Lamb Syndrome."

For some weird reason it seems to take one person coming in, no matter how good a pastor he may be, to break the memories of "the way it used to be" with the long-term pastor. This does not seem to be the case nearly so often when an acute crisis has removed the former pastor.

Inability to Move to Another Ministry

How I wish our Bible schools and seminaries would train men and women to be bivocational—tentmakers as well as preachers. When a pastor, for whatever reason, does not pastor anymore, what is a pastor to do? Sell subscriptions? I know some people who are "hangin' in there" in ministry just because they do not know what else to do, and they know that their ministry time is done. What a tragedy for all concerned.

Age can even be a filter here. We always seem to want those bright, young, articulate pastors to come and change our congregations so that we can attract the "young people," until that young whippersnapper of a pastor wants to bring about too much change. We seem to have lost the leading edge of true elders with the wisdom of the years being our mentors, our guides.

LONELINESS AND ISOLATION

The Talk Changes When the Pastor
or Pastoral Spouse Shows Up

Whenever I'm traveling on an airplane and the question comes up about work, I've found one of the quickest ways to get people to stop talking to me is to tell them I'm a minister. That is not what I am trying to do, but some people simply don't know that pastors are real people and can handle being real very well, if given the opportunity. If conversations need to change when pastors or pastoral spouses come on the scene, what was the topic of conversation anyway? Pastors are people just like you. They need relationships.

Pastors Are Not Welcome at Certain Gatherings

Ouch! Often in rural or small town settings where family groups have lived for years, or in places with a strong ethnic element, pastors and their families find it hard to "break in." Very often the pastor and family are not living close to their relatives or close friends. And I am amazed at how often pastors tell me that people simply never think to invite them to events because they think the pastor is always so busy. Your pastor is not "that" busy. If he is, something is not going right.

Neither you nor I like to be treated with exclusiveness. So invite your pastor into your circles, to your events. It might just be the relational tonic you both need without the pulpit between you.

They Hunger to Be Seen as Real Persons, Not Just Performers

One of the finest pastors I know says the pastor before him insisted on a formal relationship with the parishioners, including always being called Pastor or Reverend Jones. Now, I am all for respecting one's position, but titles distance the shepherd from his people. I know the disciples often called Jesus "Rabbi," but I'm sure they must also have been on a first name basis. I know this hits at some old traditions, but formality also separates people that were not meant to be separated. Respect is an attitude, not a title. If your pastor prefers the formal approach and you feel this sets up a barrier between you, then it's worth talking to him about it.

Another pastor I know really enjoyed fishing — and not just for men. One of the things that drew him to his particular congregation was the fact that many of the men also enjoyed outdoor activities, and when he was candidating they indicated that it was super that a pastor would enjoy the outdoors as well. But in his first four years no one went fishing with him, even when he did the inviting. Finally, one man admitted to this pastor that some of the men might be embarrassed if they uttered a cuss word or two when they didn't land a fish. Lousy excuse. It would be lovely to think that the strongest words all pastors say is, "Oh, darn," when they hit their crazy bone or don't land a fish. But let's get real. Pastors are real people.

They Can't Have Personal Problems

I actually heard a lady say, "Our pastors have no problems. We didn't hire them to have problems. If they get too many problems we just ask the district superintendent to move them, and they get moved." And I might add that the staff door at this particular church is of the revolving variety. Why? Pastors are people who have problems. The only pastors who don't are dead, and hopefully, at home with the Lord.

On a recent Sunday morning we were not able to go to church, so I took the opportunity of watching Jack Hayford's service on television. It was a powerful message, in part because he dared to be real before the world about what had angered him the week before. My wife, Judy, and I were moved by the full context of his words. Our respect for him only deepened. It was obvious he was free "to be" within that congregation. What a model for all of us. Even Jack Hayford is a "people."

They Can't Have Marital Conflicts

True or false: A minister's marriage is supposed to be a perfect example of a Christian marriage. As already expressed, to think that a pastoral marriage *must be* perfect is a sure setup for failure. To think that our pastors and their spouses are beyond conflict is not to think. To think that such good and real people as Billy and Ruth, Chuck and Cynthia, Stuart and Jill, David and Karen, Gordon and Gail, etc., have never "growled" at each other is absurd, and fortunately they have lived to tell about it.

They Can't Get Depressed

I've always liked the line that goes, "If God wanted us to be happy all the time He would have sent the Happy Spirit instead of the Holy Spirit." Some time ago, from both sides of the pulpit, we created a monster when we laid out the expectations, verbal and nonverbal, that pastors cannot have any "downside" emotions. That's depressing. Life is not all "up," not all bright days with warm, balmy breezes. Some days are the "pits" in ministry, and in life. I know a number of pastors who are depressed simply because of the loneliness and isolation they feel so acutely because their congregations do not allow them to be real, to live with the full range of human emotions.

Their Kids Can't Misbehave

One of the finest and bravest pastors I know gave his two kids permission not to attend Sunday evening church if they didn't want to. Well, some people were at first indignant because they expected the pastor's kids to set the example for their children. Nice thought. Nice idea. Not for real.

No one should be destructive or mean, but kids will be kids, just like you were once. Frankly, perfect kids are no fun. They lack spontaneity. And often preachers' kids who misbehave are only creatively yelling out that they need their parents in ways that they are not getting them.

They Can't Be Spiritually Dry

I will listen harder to pastors who tell me they have experienced spiritual dryness than to those who seem to have it all together all the time. But spiritual dryness is a fearful place to be for any of us. Yet all the great saints of the Bible experienced it. Go back and read the account of Elijah. This servant was in bad shape. It was a while before God spoke to him, even though He still provided for him. But then Elijah eventually got his "second call" from the still small voice of God high up on the side of a mountain and returned to his people.

When we are dry, it is scary. Thankfully, God is still our Abba, our Father, waiting for us to move back into His embrace. And so it will be for your pastor during a time of spiritual dryness if you allow him to be real with the ebb and flow of his life. Several books Brennan Manning has written would be important for you to read and then give to your pastor: *The Ragamuffin Gospel*, *The Signature of Jesus*, and *Abba's Child*. These will encourage anyone who is experiencing spiritual dryness.

They Are Supposed to Be Better Than the Rest of Us

Almost nothing isolates a pastor more than when we think something like that. But that is what we often think and expect, even subliminally. I know that some pastors try to play out a "role" and act like that. Just like we sometimes act better than we really are. But let's start living with the real fact that pastors are people who need what you and I need, and that is loving, caring relationships, not isolation.

PERSONAL ENCOURAGEMENT AND AFFIRMATION IN MINISTRY

Through Words and Notes

This is one of the simplest, yet most profound ways of being an encouragement. A number of months ago I visited with a solid young Christian leader in a northern state. It was interesting to see a note I had written over a year before that was tucked inside his brief-case. He held it up to me and said, "More than anything else, this single piece of encouragement has kept me anchored and focused on the Lord in the middle of the dark moments I've been facing. You will never know how timely these three sentences were when I wanted to give it all up. Thank you." It's amazing what happens when we follow God's nudges in even the simplest of activities. I'm extra thankful I took the time to send some words of encouragement to this friend, for I had no idea what he was facing in the week he received my note. Following are some more ways you can encourage your pastor through notes or words.

COMPLIMENT YOUR PASTOR. Look your pastor in the eye and tell him, "God used you in my life in that sermon (or meeting, or counseling session, or quick exchange at the ball game, or whatever) last week. This one phrase really hit home. It is good to see God using you that way."

Tell your pastor what you enjoy about his preaching. If there is not much you enjoy about his preaching, or if your pastor seems to be struggling in his preaching, think of gifting him with a full-ride scholarship (transportation, tuition, room and board) to the Dynamic Communicators Workshop held every spring in Estes Park, Colorado, for Christian leaders. I know of no finer program to help men and women improve in both their heart and skills in communicating. This would be an excellent event to send even the best of preachers to. The cost is well worth the result. For further information call 303/425-1319 or FAX 303/420-0764.

SAY IT WITH A CARD. I can't say this often enough. A well-thought-out and "felt-out" card or short letter of appreciation goes a long way on a hard day, or week, or month.

PRAY FOR AN ENCOURAGING WORD. When you are praying for your pastor or other Christian leaders in your life, ask the Lord to give you some words of encouragement for that person. I think you may be pleasantly surprised at what can fill up your mind and heart as you listen to the Spirit of God telling you what to do and say.

WRITE LETTERS OF ENCOURAGEMENT. Ever want to read someone's mail? We get the opportunity here, and a glance through our mailbag will illustrate the power of good words well spoken and/or written. One honest pastor I know and deeply respect told me how he handles such letters.

> I keep a file of "Encouraging Cards and Letters." When I'm having a tough day or am in some kind of valley of the soul, I get out that file and read through it. It reminds me that God can indeed use a weak and inadequate vessel like me.
>
> Such letters can be very creative, like the one I received the week after I had played the role of Abraham in an Easter musical: "Dear Abraham, Thank you for taking the time to visit our congregation and celebrate Easter with us. I'm ashamed to admit that I've read your story many times, yet glossed over the terrible pain and sorrow you must have felt when El Shaddai tested you to choose between Him and your beloved son, Isaac. As a father of two sons I think I can now at least begin to relate to the intense temptation and struggle that must have occurred within your soul that day on Moriah. Hopefully, you'll be able to visit again and share

additional insights from your relationship with El Shaddai. Your brother in Christ, Steve."

Or listen to the short note I received during a very painful time from someone outside our church family: "Just a note to tell you I am praying for you and to let you know that I stand ready to do anything I can. Please don't hesitate to call if you need a friendly, distant person to talk with. Run to Jesus. . . . He's the only One who can handle the pain. Keep looking up, my brother."

A support staff person wrote this in a Boss's Day card: "It has made such a difference in my working life and in my ministry to have you here. Please be assured of what a ministry of encouragement and support you and Pam have had to me and my family. Hardly a day passes that I don't thank Him for the two of you." Those kinds of things fill my file . . . and deeply encourage me.

May this man's files always be filled to overflowing! And the same for your pastor's!

FAX YOUR FORMER PASTORS. In the early hours one morning while working on this manuscript, I found the following fax in my home office. It was written by a pastoral couple who had attended a marriage preparation class I taught in 1978.

I was "cruising the net" this evening and saw your name and fax number, and I couldn't resist writing to you. . . . I thought you might be interested in hearing about how your "students" have fared so far.

One month from today will be our seventeenth wedding anniversary. . . .

We began our marriage still in college. Just to make things a little harder I became pregnant about three months into our first year of marriage. It was quite an adjustment for both of us—Tim had to change his priorities from being a "student-a-holic" to being a husband and father. I had to deal with all the normal changes of becoming a wife as well as the physical and emotional changes of pregnancy. Tim and I both had times that first year when we thought we would have a miserable marriage, because we knew we were in our marriage for better or worse, and it sure seemed like it was mostly worse! However, we were guided by the principles established in the Sunday school class, we kept communication lines open, never considered divorce, and had many wonderful times during the first year, too. . . .

Today our marriage is the most precious thing we have besides our relationship with God. Our children have all accepted Christ as their Savior and my oldest is seriously considering becoming a pastor. We certainly aren't perfect, but God has taken these clay vessels and established a loving home. God has blessed us richly, and one of those blessings was that Sunday school class years ago. Thank you for your wise, godly instruction which has borne fruit for many years in our lives. . . . May God's grace continue to abound in your work.

God knew I needed this on the very day it arrived to encourage me. It will be a "keeper" in my own file of notes and cards from over the years.

What about a pastor from your past? Which of your former pastors has impacted you in some way? What would you like to say to that pastor? What do you *need* to say to him?

COMPLIMENT THE PASTOR PUBLICLY. The more times you can publicly affirm your pastor, the better. Take him places with you and let people know that this is one of the finest ministers they could ever know.

Also, how about a church board bringing in staff members and telling them all the things they were "caught doing well" in their ministry—with no "buts"? As in, "Pastor, you are such a good, creative, challenging speaker, but sometimes you go too long." Ugh! Save the criticism for another day. Too often we humans think that if we compliment someone, we also have to deflate that person's ego immediately thereafter. Rubbish! Pay the compliment sincerely, and let it go at that.

Along the same lines, tell the pastor the good things some other member of the staff has been caught doing, and let him know you are pleased with his leadership of the staff. Don't even come close to saying this unless you are being fully truthful.

APPRECIATE YOUR PASTORAL STAFF PUBLICLY. If you are a member of the church board, take it upon yourself to get hold of the excellent Focus on the Family Pastor Appreciation materials that H. B. London and his team produce (719/531-3360). Then plan with the other board members a tremendous time of honoring your staff in a church service, at the annual Sunday school picnic, or at a formal dinner in the ballroom of a fine hotel where the sole purpose is a tribute to your pastors. Make sure it's not a roast—they get enough of that in everyday life.

CONFRONT YOUR PASTOR ONE ON ONE WITH YOUR CONCERNS. If you need to speak to your pastor about some issue of concern in your congregation, do so one on one, and be clear and concise. Don't pad your comments with compliments just to soften the blow; this warns your pastor not to trust you when you do give a sincere compliment.

ALWAYS GIVE FEEDBACK. Feedback is important for pastors. Too many of them do not get enough feedback and can consequently develop some pretty weird habits. But make certain that this feedback comes from a sincere heart of love and care about seeing that person built up to his fullest maturity in Jesus Christ. We all want to dump on folks when we are ticked—something we should not do—so allow the Spirit of God to be a tester of what you want to feed back.

TAKE YOUR PASTOR TO WORK. Invite your pastor to watch you at work, and *don't* ask him to pray. That will surprise him. Simply tell your coworkers that you very much admire your pastor and that you wanted to allow him to see what you do since you see him doing his good work every weekend.

Through Prayer

PRAY OFTEN FOR YOUR PASTOR. The Bible tells us to pray for those who have oversight of us. May those prayers begin for your pastors today. In fact, stop right now and spend a moment or two praying with whatever the Lord brings to your mind. Don't read any further. Do it right now. Then continue. Thank you, and God bless you for doing that!

We need to pray every day for our leaders. If this has not been your habit, pick one day of the week and pray much for them on that day each week. In three months, when that has become a good habit, pick a second day, and so on, until you are in the habit of praying for your pastors every day. Something will happen to your heart and theirs as you pray, and some very good things may even begin to happen in your church.

START A PASTOR'S PRAYER TEAM (PPT). I visited with a pastor friend from another state several weeks after the Promise Keepers event I mentioned at the beginning of this book. He did not attend because of a family reunion, but thirty-plus men from his congregation did.

These were his words to me:

Roberts, what happened out there in Boulder anyway? When I got home from my family reunion our lawn was mowed, the outside windows on the house were all washed, there was not a weed left in our yard.

It's my habit to go to the church every Sunday morning about six-thirty to be quiet in the sanctuary and pray for the services and for the people. Well, last Sunday when I arrived all thirty of those men were waiting for me. In fact, they were all standing in a circle holding hands and praying in the parking lot when I drove in—and you just don't do things like that in this state.

They insisted on not only praying with me, but they asked me to kneel down in front of our communion table. Then they gathered around and laid hands on me and prayed for me like I've never been prayed for in my life—and you just don't do those kinds of things in our denomination.

Then they told me they didn't want me to preach on that Sunday because they wanted to tell the rest of the people what had been going on in their lives the past two weeks since they had gotten home from Colorado. They told me how they were going to be different husbands and fathers and members of the church and the community, and that they were going to stand up for me and be with me and be praying for me and this church—and you just don't do things like that in this church.

Roberts, revival began in our little fellowship several weeks ago. And those men who have been in town have not missed praying with me on Sunday mornings since.

This good pastor then broke down and wept a bucketful of tears. When he regained some composure he said, "My life will never be the same. Nor will any life in our church. I never knew I needed prayer so badly, but I did—and do. How arrogant of me to think I could keep going alone, and then get mad when I felt so lonely."

I don't know where or when, but you need to develop a PPT for each member of your staff. In fact, you need several in your church. Men praying for men, women praying for women. And how about a prayer team for each spouse, again men praying for men and women praying for women, and everyone praying for the staff kids?

Do this at least weekly. I can't even begin to imagine the tremendous things that will be happening at your church and in all your lives. And be prepared for some real spiritual warfare as you take back the ground the enemy may have gotten, and as you plow new ground of faithfulness and service within your church and community.

Are you excited about this yet? I am!

Through Acceptance

It's interesting that what encourages one pastor may not encourage another. But being allowed to be a regular person is a core desire of genuine, authentic individuals in pastoral ministry. One pastor expressed his thoughts: "I know the church members want to honor me with the title of pastor, since I am one, but Gary is good enough for me. I don't greet people that way. I never say Teacher Jones, Homemaker Kathy, Lawyer Jim. I like hearing my name just like everyone else does. Addressing me with a title does not allow me to be real. It produces a distance that I do not want to have with my people. I know this can be cultural. But I encourage people to show their respect for us clergy by accepting us as we are, hugging us when they see us and not putting us up somewhere out of reach with a title. And besides, in one of my older translations of the Bible it says that the 'only Holy and Reverend is God.'"

That should give us something to ponder for a moment. It is interesting that pastors call each other by their first names. So do their mothers, and so does the Holy Sprit in times of sweet and quiet communion. Let's consider what we can do to let them know that we intimately accept them into our lives.

Through Involvement in the Church

FIND OUT WHAT YOU CAN DO, AND DO IT. Participation in your church life is one of the ten best ways to encourage your pastor. There *is* something there for you to do.

In fact, make an appointment with your pastor and ask either of two questions: "What do you need done that no one else is doing right now?" or "To the extent that you may know me, where do you think I can best fit in helping you with the ministry of this church?"

Take smelling salts with you, because pastors are not used to having either of these questions asked of them, and they've been known to faint dead away when these get asked. When yours wakes up, you may have to repeat the question because he will think he was dreaming.

If you are uncertain about how to do your role at church, ask for help and instruction. These days, with videos and tapes, seminars of every kind are just waiting to come to you.

Your pastor will be most encouraged by knowing that you want to grow and improve in your participation at church.

YOU'RE IN THIS TOGETHER. Don't sit back and let the pastor do all the work. Offer to do something for a month that you know the pastor (especially of a small church) has to do, but would like a break from doing, like visiting the sick in the hospital, or taking a senior citizen to the doctor, or mowing the church lawn, or changing the little plastic letters on the sign in front of the church. Let your pastor know that you are more than willing to be in this together.

TAKE LEADERSHIP. When you see something that needs doing is not getting done, take leadership. Stop waiting for someone else to do it. If something keeps coming to your mind, God may be placing that need on your own heart.

BE OPEN TO CHANGE. Do you know why there is the tradition of church services at 11:00 A.M.? Because that was between milking times in our more rural past. Let your pastor know you are willing to try new things—that will be a breath of fresh air! Encourage your church board to help the pastor try some new ways of "doing church" and let them know that you will help explain any changes to the congregation.

OFFER SERMON ASSISTANCE. Some folks love to get a copy of their pastor's preaching schedule and spend time doing research for articles, illustrations, etc., to help him in his sermon preparation. If your pastor will not let you do this for him, I know at least 198,463 other pastors who would import you tomorrow for that task.

DEVELOP A PASTORAL MINISTRY TEAM (PMT). This would be a known group in your church whose sole purpose is to know and respond to the needs of the pastors and their families—personally, in their homes, and in their ministries. These people would be able to hold a confidence, they would be there as needed, and they would stand in support of the pastors as required. This could be the most fun committee in a church, getting together and figuring out how to lavishly love and care for each pastor, spouse, and kid.

DON'T COMMITTEE YOURSELF TO DEATH. This one was suggested by a pastor I know: "Of great help to me has been our RIOT Nights (Reaching In and Out Together). We have suspended all committees but three (finance, maintenance, and missions) and have made everything else revolve around ministry teams. In one year alone we will have saved over three hundred meetings. The purpose of these nights is to give vision and evaluate ministries, leadership development, and plugging people into ministries. They are held once a quarter. No one committees themselves to death." Suggest it to your pastor.

SURPRISE THE STAFF MEETING WITH A TREAT. Bring a dozen fresh-baked cinnamon rolls by the church office on the morning of your pastoral staff weekly meeting. Swoop in, set the rolls on the table (with napkins), tell them you will be praying for them, and swoop out.

DEVELOP YOURSELF SPIRITUALLY. This may seem pretty obvious, but do all you can to grow in your own personal relationship with the triune God. I can guarantee you that you will encourage your pastor as he sees Jesus alive in you. Also, come to Sunday service with an open heart and mind ready to receive from God. This way the pastor does not have to fight to bring the Lord's Word to you.

REMEMBER WHO YOU ARE SERVING. When you do have some task within your church, seen by all or known only to God, don't forget *who* you are doing it for in the first place. If you kept this in mind, any and all service within your church would be done with an excellence and diligence that would be so uplifting for your pastor, for your friends at church, for yourself, and most of all, for Him.

Through Accountability

We discussed accountability in chapter 2, "Personal Life of the Pastor," but it is important enough to mention again, with different applications for the pastor in ministry. Every minister—indeed, every person—needs to be in accountable relationships outside the home. We all need to be asked the hard questions and confronted on our life issues.

Pastors find it hard to open up and be vulnerable. They have carefully learned how to protect themselves; many live lonely lives, even in the midst of a lot of church activity. Pastors find it hard to open up from a fear of rejection and from wondering what people are going to think. But a pastor must overcome this if he is going to be a healthy, growing pastor and finish well in ministry, and in life.

Pastors need to be encouraged to be accountable to members of their same sex, and not just to their spouse. Being the sole accountability person for the pastor, the spouse bears incredible pressure that the pastoral marriage was not meant to have. Needed in each pastor's life are people who will love him, who can be objective, and who are true friends, able to be trusted.

CONSIDER A "PASTORAL ADVISORY BOARD." This is a hand-picked group of church leaders who help the pastor stay on track. Their primary purposes are encouragement, accountability (mutually agreed on—this is not the parole board), and wise counsel. They can help the pastor avoid burnout, bad decisions, and loss of focus. This group can also offer input on balancing family and ministry, conflict resolution, matters of the heart, etc. The key is that these be solid people whom the pastor feels can be trusted, can be open, and will be supportive.

START A WEEKLY PRAYER GROUP. Insist may be too strong a term, but almost insist that your pastor meet with a group of men weekly for prayer. Volunteer to lead it.

TRY THE "ELDER-A-WEEK BREAKFAST CLUB." Every week one of the elders takes the pastor out to breakfast just to be with him, to share "what's new" and pray for him—not to receive personal counseling. Set up that schedule and sign up now.

ALLOW THE PASTOR TO SHOW HIS HURT. This is sober, but good. Some forms of accountability in churches are more destructive than helpful. These forms force the pastor to take cover and fake it instead of giving him the opportunity to be real and vulnerable. Each church needs a system for allowing the pastor to show his hurt. What would that system look like in your church?

ENCOURAGE BIBLICAL COUNSELING. I recommend that Christian leaders go through about six months of solid biblical counseling every three to five years, crisis or not, just to talk through some of the deeper issues of the heart. Those who do not do this are not living well somewhere in their lives. Those who do seek godly, intense counsel are found to be thriving very well. Encourage your pastor to take this opportunity.

ENSURE THAT THE PASTOR GETS TIME OFF. Almost the worst thing a pastor can say is, "I haven't had a day off in a month." That's sinful! Make certain your pastor takes his regular time off. Make it part of your ministry at church. If his day off gets invaded, help him find some new time off. This is critical!

RETOOL FOR ACCOUNTABILITY. Encourage a board member to meet once a month with each pastor in your church and ask the pastors these questions. Make certain they are asked in a same-gender context.

▶ What has been your greatest struggle in ministry since we last met together?
▶ Is there a burden in your life right now that I could pray about?
▶ What is the most encouraging thing that has happened to you since we last met?
▶ What kind of help do you need right now?

▶ How are your personal finances? In what ways are you worrying about money?

▶ How is your spouse handling the stress of the ministry emotionally?

Those are good questions to retool for any accountability time with a good friend.

Through Respect and Support

STAND UP FOR YOUR PASTOR WHEN HE IS NOT PRESENT TO DEFEND HIMSELF.

BE A PEACEMAKER. Pastors get a ton of criticism every week. When you know he is under the gun, let him know you are standing with him. Jesus did say, "Blessed are the peacemakers."

HELP YOUR PASTOR R.U.N. FROM TEMPTATION!

R

▶ *Remind* him often of his promises.

▶ Include a renewal of his wedding vows as a part of his installation service and incorporate his children into the service.

▶ Include a renewal of his ordination vows as part of a yearly anniversary or on a special church anniversary.

U

▶ *Undergird* his life and family with prayer.

▶ Consider Peter Wagner's *Prayer Shield* or Glen Martin and Dian Ginter's *Drawing Closer: A Step-By-Step Guide to Intimacy with God* and *Power House: A Step-By-Step Guide to Building a Church That Prays* for ideas of how to pray for the pastor and his family.

▶ Encourage a "family a day" rotation of praying for your pastor as part of the membership requirements for your church.

N

- ▶ *Nurture* his life and family with practical expressions of love.
- ▶ Write a job description that contracts a consistent day at home, the number of evenings at home per week, the number of dates out with wife per month, etc.
- ▶ Allow pastors with young kids to begin work at noon when the previous evening is committed.
- ▶ Have a "pastor weekend" away at vacation homes Sunday through Monday.

Through Relationship

GET ALONG. Encourage your pastor by getting along with your brothers and sisters in Christ. Then he won't have to expend time and energy putting out fires.

TRY BEING LESS CRITICAL. Stop talking behind the pastor's back. Do not be part of any bad mouthing toward your pastor. That is not right, no matter how much one can justify such behavior. Are you really speaking the truth or just your version of the truth? Is love your motivation? Settle that with God first, before you open your mouth.

HELP THE PASTOR WITH THE CRITICISM HE RECEIVES. Offer to be a buffer, absorber, mediator for him with disgruntled church members (do this and you are on your way to instant sainthood). If someone has unresolved anger over some issue, do something kind for that person: take him to dinner, have him over for coffee, play golf, and listen, listen, listen.

Often the best question you can ask a disgruntled person is, "Anything else?" Keep asking that question until he has nothing more to say. Then ask that person's permission to share with him your larger vision for the church. That may answer some of his concerns. If he is not satisfied with that, then bring others in at another time to listen well, dialogue with him, and pray with him. Interesting things can happen when there is earnest and sincere prayer about disagreements. We can trust Him for that.

IF YOU HAVE A DISAGREEMENT. Don't be afraid to give your pastor feedback. And if you disagree with your pastor, have the courage to speak to him calmly and in control. Listen long and hard to what he is really saying. Then ask clarifying questions so that both of you know what you are talking about, even if you still disagree. To disagree is okay, to be disagreeable is not. This will help you work on issues together before there is a gaping wound.

If you have had a particularly difficult board or congregational meeting with the pastor, invite him out for coffee and *don't* talk about church, unless he needs to.

Also, don't dump your disagreements on the pastor before a service or in between services. If it is truly that important, make an appointment as a civilized and caring person would do and see him during the week.

Defeat the enemy often. When he tries to put bitterness between you and your pastor, make the first move to set it right.

ALWAYS SIGN YOUR NOTES. Never, *never*, *NEVER* send a note to your pastor without a signature. If you have a legitimate suggestion or complaint, speak to him personally and privately. I tell Christian leaders the world over not to pay attention to anything that comes unsigned. I tell them to throw it away. It's not worth keeping around, unless it is a threat of physical violence. Sorry to say, but that is not unusual in this day and age.

ROLE/MINISTRY EXPECTATIONS

Financial

PAY YOUR PASTOR WELL. Simply stated, most pastors are not paid enough. My suggestion is that the *beginning* salary for all members of a pastoral staff should be 20 percent above the average salary in your congregation. It should compare favorably with those of similar professionals in your community (psychologists, professors, executive directors, etc.). Adjustments need to be made according to true need, not just length of time at the church, education, experience, etc. For example, if any of your pastoral staff has to rent, make certain that increases in rent are reflected in salary raises.

One young pastor's wife said, "Provide an adequate salary so that my husband will be able to do what the average person at the church does. For example, we cannot afford to put our kids in the sports and music programs that are a huge deal in our town. Could someone give a special gift to make that possible for our kids?"

We are responsible for meeting well the needs of those who minister to us.

PROVIDE ADEQUATE BENEFITS IN EVERY AREA. It is vital that you provide adequately in health insurance, life insurance, and retirement. Don't always buy health plans or insurance for your pastors from a member of your congregation. Go shopping! You could still end up buying it from that member, but look for what is best for your pastors, with certainty. Besides, insurance people understand the competitive nature of their business.

Make certain that your health care plan for your staff is more than adequate. To keep costs down, get a high deductible plan, *but* provide for full reimbursement for that and for other medical expenses. Covering the deductible expenses in a thousand-dollar deductible is cheaper than providing a lesser deductible, but the major coverage for catastrophes will still be there.

If you are in a small church that does not have the luxury of extra monies for good benefits and other compensation, consider a network of small-church pastors who can form co-ops and use combined resources to help one another.

REVIEW SALARY AND BENEFITS ANNUALLY. In these changing times, make certain your board reviews the salary and benefit package annually. Please sit down with both the pastor *and* spouse to do this. Encourage them to hold back nothing, and then give them more than they were expecting. Taking time to talk with them in this way shows, almost more than anything else, that you care about their well-being.

CHECK YOUR TITHES AND OFFERINGS. This could be a novel thought for some, but how about making certain that your personal level of tithes and offerings are up to date for your church? This will allow your church to care for your pastors properly.

PROVIDE MONEY FOR RETREATS, BANQUETS, ETC., THAT WOULD NORMALLY COME OUT OF THE PASTOR'S POCKET.

BE MINDFUL OF INEQUITIES. On one hand, be careful with precedents. On the other, get into the practice of loving well your staff through how you take care of them financially. I know that a weird message is sent to the "junior staffers" when the senior pastor receives help for buying his home and a similar generosity does not apply to the rest of the pastoral team.

The inequities between senior and staff positions make for a lot of resentment sometimes among staff spouses. It would be great if a church would look not just at seniority and position, but also at reasonable needs. If the spouse has to work because the church is not able to pay adequately, then that spouse needs to have lighter expectations about what she can do around the church.

Speaking of spouses, members of the board should think about doing a review of the staff spouses, *not* for their performance but to make certain that *all* their needs are being met.

PROVIDE FOR STAFF FUNCTIONS. Senior pastors need to spend personal time with their staff and spouses for a rollicking good time and some sort of checkup on how things are going. Do you have a mountain or lake cabin that could work for that? Or could you invite them all over to your home for a swim and a cookout and leave them alone to talk among themselves? Or how about giving them all two nights away together in another town at a bed and breakfast, with the intent to talk things out among themselves and build bonds between them.

Job Description
THE PRIMARY COMPONENTS. Do *all* you can to make certain that praying (being often before the Father, Son, and Holy Spirit),

preaching/teaching (time in the Word), and giving spiritual direction (being with the people often) are the three primary components of a pastor's job description.

THEY MUST BE FLUID AND RELEVANT. Most job descriptions are either so general, so archaic, or so grandiose that the apostle Paul would not know exactly what was required of him. Remember, this is not a business, this is a church, a fellowship of believers we are concerned about. Job descriptions need to reflect the expectations of all of a pastor's life — at the church, in the community, and at home, since ministry is a twenty-nine-hour-a-day deal. Do the job descriptions truly state what is actually happening? Have they been changed from pastor to pastor? They need to be, for an adequate job description should reflect not only the "must haves" of the position, but it must also reflect the unique gifts and talents of this particular person. I could say a lot more about this area, so contact me if you want to know more. Job descriptions need to state the facts and significantly decrease unrealistic expectations.

DELEGATE TASKS. What can others do that the pastor would not like to do, or is not skilled in doing? Most pastors, bless 'em, are not good administrators. That's not a count against them; that is not what God has called them to do in their pastoral role. Perhaps someone recently retired with experience in management could assume those responsibilities. If your church is big enough, take this burden off your pastor and hire a full-time administrator to work for and with your pastor. Even if the position is part-time, those will be wise dollars, well spent.

I have a very good friend who, other than his personal administrative assistant, had all volunteer help in the church office, coordinated by a retired executive secretary. They got things done in this church of about nine hundred people. How could you volunteer to help your pastor in this way?

HOLD A PASTORAL NEEDS MEETING. This could be a scary thought to most pastors, but it also could be a great lesson in trust.

It will take some planning with the church board. Suggest that there be a congregational meeting where anything negative will *not* be a topic of conversation (right there we could be instigating a miracle!). What will be talked about is understanding *all the needs* within the church in every area of church life and with the duties of the pastoral and support staff. Then the members sign up for what they will do for the next twelve months to help carry the load. Ephesians 4 speaks extra clearly that one of the primary roles of the pastor is to equip the saints to carry on the ministry of the church. That's you and me. Careful, this could really be fun, if you truly allowed the Spirit of God to punch your creativity buttons.

HOLY GRIPING. Give your pastors and other staff a chance to do some "holy griping." Give them the opportunity to type a series of three-by-five cards with their "top ten" list of ministry frustrations within the whole church. Then—O Holy Spirit, be with these people who are this courageous!—without being defensive get the leadership together to talk about these issues and arrive at mutually acceptable solutions. It's my hope that there would be enough growth and maturity eventually to know who wrote what, so specific attention can be paid to the particular foxes that are spoiling your church vines.

LET THE CHURCH BOARD DECIDE. As best you can, have all church decisions approved and implemented by the church board. Criticism can thus be shared rather than directed solely at the pastor. This calls for careful announcements of implementation and restraint in waiting for the whole board to make the wise decisions they are supposed to make.

ENCOURAGE OUTSIDE CONSULTATION. Encourage your pastor to bring in an outside consultant occasionally to help you objectively evaluate the ministry of your church. Check chapter 6 for suggestions, especially our own ministry, Life Enrichment.

Expectations

ADOPT THESE THREE PRIORITIES AS THE FOCUS OF THE
MINISTRY OF YOUR CHURCH:

- ▶ A growing commitment to Jesus Christ
- ▶ A growing commitment to the body of Christ
- ▶ A growing commitment to the work of Jesus Christ in the
  world

LET YOUR PASTOR KNOW YOU DO NOT EXPECT HIM TO HAVE
ALL THE ANSWERS. Offer to pray for or with him and seek out
answers to issues in his life and/or the congregation's.

LIST THE EXPECTATIONS. For too many pastors, expectations get
defined as what they wish their church had told them before they
took the job in comparison to the reality of what can be done once
they get there. Therefore, when you call a new pastor, have the congregation make up a very specific list of expectations for the position. Then ask for a similar list from the person you may want to call,
his spouse, and his kids. Nothing is worse than hidden agendas or
expectations surfacing after a person has been called to a new ministry.

FIGHTING WORKAHOLISM. Workaholism is a pastoral disease.
The demands of the ministry in most churches are so great that it is
easy for a pastor to become a workaholic at the expense of his family. Encourage him to have balance in his life and help him see it if
he doesn't. *Please*, do all you can to make certain that your pastors
have time for their families.

I like these words from a staff pastor: "The senior pastor told
me that the elders said if I don't take a vacation, they are going to
lock the church doors on me. One of them volunteered their condo
for our family, and they all took a collection and gave us some
spending money and money for gas." Good for those elders!

NO UNINVITED EXPECTATIONS. This is good admonition for us
all from a dear saint I know: "I think sometimes pastors and mis-

sionaries are put up on a pedestal and the expectation is for them to be 'more holy' or have it all together. When we place uninvited expectations upon someone in leadership, we will no doubt be disappointed. No one is perfect. And in my opinion Satan will attack those in leadership more because they are having an impact on people's spiritual lives. Perhaps the biggest encouragement we can offer is our *lack* of judging our pastors! Let them be people who make mistakes just like we do. But rather than sitting back smugly and smiling about it, be the prayer warrior who is in the gap for them on a daily basis."

THE QUESTION OF TIME OFF. Encourage your pastor to have set office hours, and encourage church members to respect those hours and not bother the pastor at home.

Everyone in the church should know when the pastor takes his day off. This is his personal sabbatical. *Do not disturb!* Everyone in the congregation needs to understand that the pastor should be called on those days only in case of an emergency, and then to go through his secretary or a board member.

Frankly, time out, days off, for a pastor is a mutual responsibility between the pastor and the congregation. For some reason, most people in helping professions are not good at self-care and drawing their own boundaries because they always see the needs of hurting people out there. But be willing to tackle this head-on and insist that your pastor talk over with someone the need for time out and self-care. Chapter 6 can help you both in this. This is of critical importance!

Having been in full-time ministry since 1965, and in this specific ministry to Christian leaders since 1982, I have formed some opinions about a pastor's time off, no matter what the size of the church or the seniority of the individual.

If you have the right staff people in the right positions for your congregational needs, I believe all staff in pastoral positions, ordained or not, seminary degree or not, need to be given equal time off at the very least. If more time is required according to unusual need, then give it to them without penalty or envy.

You ask, "What exactly do you have in mind?"

I'm glad you asked! You must be a person of tremendous insight and foresight who *really* does love your pastors.

Sincerely, I see this *not* working only if you had the wrong people in the wrong position and if, for some reason, you did not trust the people you did have in place. Pastors — good ones — are "on duty" twenty-four hours a day. All the more reason that time off needs to be given as a gift of great intentionality.

At the minimum, one day off per week. That means a full twenty-four hours with *no* church involvement — to rest, recreate, renew, spend time with the spouse and kids; to do what needs to be done around the house that no church member has come by to do (some pastors do like to garden and wallpaper as a hobby, so don't be offended if they say no to one of your offers). This needs to be a time when the pastor does whatever he wants. This is vital to the ongoing health of every pastor! If that time is interrupted with any emergency church involvement, then another twenty-four-hour time frame needs to be rescheduled to begin this process all over again. Of course, do this reasonably. You can't give the guy a day off per emergency phone call. But do get intentional and creative here.

Four weeks of vacation per year for every pastoral person. Where did we ever get the idea that our pastors' time off should be a reward for time put in, like, "Hey, Pastor, you seem tired again this week. Why don't you take some time off and get your perspective back?" That is a good idea, but for those in ministry it is a bit backward.

How about time off so that the time put in can be at its best? We all need rest when we are weary. But too often with the issue of rest we are living reactively rather than proactively. Therefore, I am suggesting four weeks of vacation per year, to be divided into two time frames: one two-week period in the first half of the year, another in the second half. If I were an elder or deacon or member of your church board, I would rarely approve of pastors taking the whole time in one lump. Their vacations need to be stretched out throughout the year. They can hold on if they know relief is coming soon.

☞*One week of personal or couple renewal every year (or more, as needed).* Do not let your pastor read this next story, or he will want to move.

There is a church in the United States that began in 1993 under the direction of one of the finest groups of people you could know. As the steering committee of this new fellowship gathered to pray and trust the Lord for the development of their church, one of the items that became high priority was a commitment to the health and strength of every pastoral couple and family. The head of the steering committee affirmed that they wanted to make certain right from the beginning that staff couples had an annual checkup of some sort, just the two of them. They wanted their time at that church to strengthen their marriage and not deplete it in any way. They made a yearly retreat part of the budget.

I only wish there were more churches willing to be so bold, so courageous, so caring, and so insightful as Lake Valley Community Church in Hot Springs, Arkansas. The dividends of this kind of care are being seen weekly as this body of believers continues to grow and flourish in a place where it can be hard to grow a church.

Every pastoral couple needs a week out like this annually. This is not to be counted as vacation time, study leave time, or a leave of absence. It is a time for that couple to pay attention to their own issues, their own hearts, their own relationship. And this does not have to be a time of "heavy counseling," though if that is needed, I recommend some exceptional places in chapter 6. But it does need to include a time with some sort of consultant or counselor or spiritual director who can give some guidance and gentle structure to the hours. It can be a time of much rest, and there needs to be some time for recreation and play.

☞*One week, or more, of annual study leave.* I believe that man of the cloth needs an annual dose of spiritual rejuvenation. It may be a quiet time away at a spiritually directed retreat center. You may send them off to the Moody Pastors' Conference, held every spring in Chicago, sponsored by Moody Bible Institute. This is a challenging, stimulating, wonderful annual event. (I just read what I wrote, and if you do have a "moody" pastor, he probably does need to be sent somewhere.) If your church is part of a denomination or church association, check into what is offered. The Navigators, at their Glen Eyrie Conference Center in Colorado Springs, also present a fine series of programs for those in ministry. Call 719/598-1212 for more information. Again, check chapter 6 for more suggestions.

It is here I would allow educational involvement. Consult with the pastor about what additional training he needs to be at his very best, and lead the charge to get him those opportunities. One option would be formal education at an approved seminary. One pastor told me he works toward some sort of degree or certification, rather than just attending random seminars.

Find out what program will encourage your pastor the most in his walk with God. Do all you can to get him to the right place for the needs of his heart, and pray for him daily while he is gone. Except for gender-specific conferences, make provision with funds and baby-sitting so that the spouse can attend seminars also, but let the two of them determine if the spouse will go. Spouses often need the refreshment and uplift even more than the pastor.

Sabbatical time every six to ten years. I am amazed, appalled, and chagrined at the number of churches that have not considered an adequate policy for sabbaticals for members of their church staff. It's a concept as old as the Bible, since the idea came from God first. It is a concept with purpose.

Such a policy needs to come down to what is best for your church. In today's rush through life and ministry, this is, in general, what I would suggest. Tweaking these thoughts for your own unique fellowship is easy. Getting your board to see them as a biblical response to staff ministry is sometimes a little harder. However, where boards have dared to adopt this policy, and the others mentioned, you have very alive and excited pastoral staffs who are working well in a trusted and nurturing environment.

I would suggest that the sabbatical be no fewer than four months and no longer than six months. This cannot be scientifically proven, but it seems to take a pastor with this gift of time several weeks to relax, to finally believe he doesn't have to be at the church on Sundays. Then it takes another few weeks for the pastor's body to believe it is functioning by a different time schedule and can engage in recreation almost anytime it wants to. Then it takes the pastor's mind a few more weeks to rest easy about not thinking heavy theological thoughts all the time, but to just enjoy what God brings to mind as the breezes blow and the clouds float by. And then it takes the pastor's heart a few more weeks to be strong and quiet enough to listen to the still small voice of almighty God, to engage in renewal, and just maybe some revival. And then . . . it's time to rethink one's call and return with refocused vision to the place God has led him to live out His call in his life.

Did you get those R's of a sabbatical? Relax. Recreation (fun, play). Rest. Renewal. Revival. Rethinking. Refocusing. Return. These are the elements of an honest, biblical sabbatical.

A biblical sabbatical is not going off to earn a degree. If that is what your pastor wants to do, then work out the details for him to do it. But this is not the kind of sabbatical I'm talking about. It is strenuous work going off and gaining some more education, and a lofty and worthy goal if God is in it.

A biblical sabbatical is not going off to write a book. If that is what your pastor needs to do, then carefully craft how he will use his writing time and his ministry time to accomplish that task. But this is not the kind of sabbatical I'm talking about. Writing is a time-consuming task, and a good one if God is in it.

A biblical sabbatical is not going off on a mad dash to visit the forty-seven most successful churches in North America. If that is what your pastor needs to do, then let him go see how others are doing the work of the ministry. But this is not the kind of sabbatical I'm talking about. It can be stimulating and rewarding to see how other pastors are leading their churches, if God is in it.

What is a good, solid, life-changing, restorative, biblical sabbatical? One where the pastor relaxes, recreates (plays), rests, is renewed and revived, rethinks the dimensions of his life, refocuses, and returns ready to serve the King of kings with refreshment and grace. These are the elements of an honest, biblical sabbatical.

"Good night!" you say. "That's six weeks off a year, plus that much time off every few years! Do you think we're made of money or something at our church? Are you serious?"

Relax. I can count. And yes, I am serious.

I am serious because of what I see happening to clergy across our world who are not given, or don't take, the time to get away and get renewed in every dimension of their lives. The "crash and burn" effects may not show up for years — good people, especially type-A sorts, can hide this well — but ultimately pastors always do crash and burn in subtle to awful ways, if they do not take the time off and the time out they need daily, weekly, monthly, quarterly, annually. There must have been some reason that God instituted a Sabbath rest. He must have known that the extreme busyness of this century was on its way. You can only blame me for tweaking His ideas into a format that fits our times.

If I were any more serious, we would be having this conversation in person instead of just through the pages of a book. Your pastors need this kind of time, *if* they are in the right positions, doing the Lord's work in the right ways. Jesus was always hiking off to the hills to spend time with His Father to get rested, recreated, and renewed for the next round of ministry. If we truly want our pastors following Jesus, then we can expect no less of them.

If we sincerely want our pastors to finish well in both their lives and ministries, then I think we need to pay close attention to all that I have just suggested. Form a sabbatical committee to listen to the heart and needs of the pastor. This special group can help formulate the plans and raise any additional funds for travel or other extra expenses for the pastor and family (I'm assuming that you know that his regular salary goes on as usual, just as his monthly needs do) and assure the church that all will be well with the pastor gone for this period of time. I would be happy to dialogue further with you on this important and necessary issue.

HOW DOES GOD DEFINE SUCCESS IN MINISTRY? This is a great discussion question for your church board, Bible study group, prayer group, or with those to whom you are accountable. It is not an easy question to answer. After you discuss it, ask your pastor what he thinks, and let him know what your group decided. You all need to know the answers for your church anyway so that you can properly support your local pastor.

WHAT DO THEY NEED WHEN HURTING? Ask other pastors you know what they need when they are hurting, when things are not going quite right at home, when they are discouraged. Then ask your pastor if that fits what he needs. This is a great way to let your pastor know you care.

PERSONAL DEVELOPMENT

Through His Involvement Away from the Church

ENCOURAGE NETWORKING. Give your pastor permission and encourage him to be part of a network of pastors to discuss issues related to the ministry as well as problem-solve and receive support from those who know the "true truth" of the pastorate.

PROVIDE TIME FOR CHURCH VISITING. Allow the pastor to attend other churches in the community or around the country to see what helpful, creative things they may be doing.

SEND YOUR PASTOR ON AT LEAST ONE MISSIONS TRIP EVERY OTHER YEAR. Don't count this as any sort of vacation time. The ministry time away will be intense and blessed. If you can afford it, send another staff person with him.

ALLOW FOR COMMUNITY OPPORTUNITIES. Allow your pastor the time to be involved in community groups or on the school board, to attend city council meetings (and not just to pray), to be a presence in your town.

SEND THE PASTOR ON A TRIP. Israel may be where he wants to go for his fifteenth anniversary at the church, but it could instead be a golf camp in Scottsdale, Arizona. Check with him in some manner before you give him the "trip of a lifetime." Don't forget what his spouse may find of interest as well.

Through Reading and Study Time

SUGGEST A DEVOTIONAL BOOK THAT HAS HAD AN IMPACT ON YOU.

ENCOURAGE READING. Give your pastor a coupon for a good novel or a trivia book—no theology, psychology, or business "stuff" allowed. For serious books, though, you may want to arrange for an annual book allowance for each of your pastors.

BE LIBERAL IN MAGAZINE SUBSCRIPTIONS. Don't ask the whole staff to share one copy of *Leadership Journal*. Let every member of your pastoral team have a subscription. You wouldn't believe how many churches go cheap on little things like this.

ENCOURAGE REST AND READING. Encourage your pastor to find a quiet place once a quarter (like Fairhaven in Tennessee—see chapter 6) and go alone for three or four days and do nothing but read and rest. He'll think he's died and gone to heaven, especially if you or a Sunday school class or the men's prayer group pays for such a retreat.

For shorter stints, if the church offices are not the best place to study and be alone, find a cottage or a home where no one is present during the day. Help the pastor get away from office interruptions.

DON'T SKIMP ON PREPARATION TIME. How long does it take your pastor to prepare the message of his dreams? Preparation time is critical for teaching pastors, so make certain the board gives him adequate time to prepare. Fifteen to twenty hours a week would be a good target to aim for.

ENCOURAGE PERSONAL PRAYER AND BIBLE STUDY. Encourage your pastor to take time each day for prayer and personal Bible study that is not related to his message, but just for his own spiritual renewal. Let him know you will be praying for that time. If he can be encouraged to make that a consistent time, like 9:00 to 11:00 A.M., the congregation needs to know so no one calls during those hours.

Through Provision of Equipment, Space, and Support Personnel

MAKE CERTAIN THE FURNITURE AND MATERIALS IN YOUR PASTORAL AND SUPPORT STAFF OFFICES ARE RIGHT FOR YOUR PASTORS.

▶ Do the chairs fit? Do the bucket seats fit the "buckets" of the staff?
▶ Is the lighting easy on the eyes?
▶ Is the space cool and warm when it should be at the correct times of year?
▶ Are the bookshelves adequate?
▶ Is it a pleasant, attractive, bright place to live several hours a day?
▶ Is there a place for, or are the offices conducive to, confidential counseling?
▶ Are there enough filing cabinets for each member of the staff—with locks?
▶ Is your computer system adequate?
▶ Does each pastor have his own computer or lap-top?
▶ Is your phone system the best it can be?
▶ Is the supply closet filled weekly with the materials everyone needs?
▶ Does your church have an e-mail system? I would heartily recommend one for the church office, and for each of your pastors as well. You may want to give them an e-mail allowance. Let your pastors know you will pay their monthly e-mail fee.

PROVIDE SOUND SYSTEMS AND TAPES. Set up a small, quality, personal sound system in the office of each pastor and give him a selection of worship CDs and other favorite music. There are some great systems that can fit easily on a bookshelf, and the sound is excellent.

SUPPORT HELP. If your pastor does not have an administrative assistant or personal secretary, make this a high staffing priority with your church board. It is amazing to me how many pastors in some very good churches do not have adequate support help. This is not a luxury. It is a necessity.

Most pastors have not been trained to work well with assistants. If you have a good administrative assistant where you work, ask if he or she would be willing to tutor your pastor and his assistant in the fine art of working well together.

Through Resources That Encourage Growth

BE A CHANNEL OF ILLUSTRATIONS. One pastor wrote to me, "I appreciate people who are a channel of illustrations to me." Go and do likewise.

GIVE TAPES. If your pastor genuinely has the time to listen to them, give him good tapes—secular or Christian—to feed him and encourage him in his work. One of the best series I know about is from John Maxwell's ministry, INJOY. Subscribe for your pastor to the INJOY LIFE CLUB, an excellent series on leadership issues. Call 800/333-6506 for further information. This is good material for you as well in your business or professional life as a Christian leader.

CHAPTER

5

FOR PASTORS TO PONDER ABOUT THEMSELVES

(AND FOR PEW SITTERS TO EAVESDROP ON)

Hopefully between the two of us (assuming you are a pastor reading this), we can figure out a way to get this book into the hands of as many of your people as possible. It is my deepest hope that your entire board, and others in your congregation who enjoy serving Jesus well, will take to heart what has been suggested and just do it. My life is committed to seeing Christian leaders, like yourself, strengthened in all your relationships—with your Lord, personally within yourself, in your home, in your life-work, and in your leisure. This book is one step in that direction.

But this book would not be complete without a word to you who so faithfully minister day after day in many ways that are known only to God. These words from my mind and heart are flying into my computer the day after a lengthy conversation with one of my best friends, a pastor with whom you would be proud to be associated. He is less than two years into a new ministry, a good ministry. He was ten years in his last pastorate where God used him in significant ways.

I have a deep, deep concern for my friend. In a phone conversation with his wife yesterday I heard the weariness in her voice with regard to his schedule. She is one of the finer pastors' wives on the face of the earth. Pastor and wife are very much partners in the ministry they do. But over recent months I've begun to be extra concerned for them.

We all live with stress. The only people who don't are not breathing but decaying. The tragedy is that some people are still breathing, and also decaying.

I once heard stress in life equated to a rubber band. If you string a rubber band around a stack of papers and leave it there, stretched to the max for a long, long time, when you attempt to remove the band from that pile of papers, often the rubber band breaks. We've all had that happen. But if you take a rubber band of fair quality and stretch it, then relax it, then stretch it, then relax it, then stretch it, then relax it, you can do that for a long time without the rubber band breaking. A good rubber band on permanent stretch develops cracks and fissures, imperceptible at first. But as the cracks grow bigger and the band weaker, it takes only the slightest pressure to snap, and the contents that were held together go flying in all directions.

My pastor friend mentioned above is one bright man with a deep love for his Lord and for his people. Because I love him like a close brother, I can say that he is getting tarnished and less bright in the category of taking care of himself. I do not like that, and told him so last night. The best and the worst among us can snap if we do not make the necessary changes in our lives.

Everyone I know, me included, has that potential. But one of the main problems in the pastorate is that there are seldom times of letting our "rubber-banded life" get away from the stretch. Then, no matter whether you are a rural pastor, a suburban pastor, an inner city pastor, a "top gun" in your particular church group, well known in your service or known only to God, life for you will snap someday in some way. I do not want to see that for you. It does not have to happen.

I do not want to see my close, longtime friend snap. This friend, who is a pastor in a growing church in a great city and is one of the "good guys" in our country when it comes to thinking about who the good pastors are, has somehow been blinded to his own plight. His staff and the people in his church think he is awesome. In so many ways he is. His calling is evident. His giftings are certain. He is one of those men you would want to be your pastor. But his personal rubber band is stretched about as far as it can go, and has been for far too long.

Pastors in crisis have tragically been characterized in the life and times of Jim and Tammy Bakker. One more time they were paraded before the world on several pages in the April 6, 1992, issue of *People Magazine*. This sad chapter in their personal history had Tammy divorcing Jimmy and taking up with their best friend from Wichita, Roe Messner. I quote from the article:

> In January they (Roe and his wife) separated. "Today," says a family friend, "Roe has every intention of marrying Tammy Faye." "I think he believes he's in love with her," confirms Ruth Ann (Roe's wife) with dry — and angry — humor. "Any man who would want Tammy Faye is not the man for me."

But he may be the man for Tammy Faye. "All Tammy ever wanted was for Jim to care about her, to pay attention to her," says Don Hardister, who was Bakker's bodyguard for twelve years. Yet from early on, many church colleagues say, Jim was more interested in his ministry than his marriage— and Tammy had to learn to tend to her own needs.

This celebrated tragedy in ministry was deeply felt by the Bakker children. They were quoted in the last paragraph of the *People* article:

"Mother and Dad are real people," says the Bakker's son, Jamie, 16. "Bad things happen to real people. We'll make the best of it." His sister, Tammy Sue, 22, who had agreed to take the helm of the Jim and Tammy ministry until her father returns, echoes her brother's beleaguered optimism. "I love my mom and dad so much," she sobbed in her first official sermon March 15 to a half-empty room of concerned Christians and curious Orlando tourists. "The devil has tried to hurt us in so many ways. [But] we are not going to give up. We will grow. Something good is going to happen."

You can have your own opinion about the whole Bakker debacle. We've laughed (sort of) with Carson, Letterman, and Leno about the whole affair. We've cringed (some) whenever "these kinds of people" get caught up once more in the news. But to much of the general population, such antics from these and other well-known religious/Christian figures have tainted how people think of pastors in our society.

The Bakkers in life do not need our scorn—they need our prayers. You and I do not need the scorn of others either. And heaven knows we need the prayers of those who truly care.

Clear back in the May 17, 1985, issue of *Christianity Today*, in a thought-provoking article titled "The Problems of Battered Pastors," Marshall Shelley reported the following:

Pastoral roles have multiplied in recent years. "I find very few individuals with an unrealistic expectation of the pastor—it's the composite image that gets to you," said one Congregational pastor. "Each person expects something different. And rarely does anyone outside the pastoral family see the composite."

What is this composite? The servant-shepherd quietly meeting personal needs without regard for personal acclaim. The prophet-politician dominating local headlines while fighting for truth and justice. The preacher-enthraller attracting the unchurched with entertaining, uplifting sermons. The teacher-theologian challenging the most serious Bible student with verse-by-verse "meat" of the Word. The evangelist-exhorter winning converts through both private conversation and public crusade. The organizer-promoter administering an effective Christian education program, music ministry, and social activities for all ages. The caller-comforter visiting the sick, consoling the bereaved, playing checkers with the lonely. The counselor-reconciler offering guidance to the distressed, therapy for the disturbed, mediation for those in dispute, and restoration for the divorced. The equipper-enabler personally training motivated laypeople to serve, prophesy, preach, teach, evangelize, organize, call, and counsel.

Here's another look at what has been reported about pastors. Hank Whittemore wrote a lengthy article for *Parade Magazine* under the title, "Ministers Under Stress." His opening paragraphs get our attention:

> Members of Atlanta's prestigious Wieuca Road Baptist Church were shocked last year when their long-time pastor, Dr. William Self, then 58, announced that he was resigning because the stress of the job had become too much for him. "Unless I quit now," he told them, "my obituary will read, 'Bill Self today sank like a rock—beat up, burned out, angry and depressed, no good to himself, no good to the people he loved.'"

For more than a quarter of a century, Dr. Self had been seemingly tireless as a preacher, teacher, minister, counselor, fund-raiser and administrator. What gradually wore him down, he says, was "subconsciously navigating into the age-old 'walk on water' syndrome—the notion that, because you're a preacher, you can accomplish anything."

"I did not have a crisis of faith, but of emotion and energy," he says. "It's almost impossible for leaders of a congregation to accept that their pastor needs pastoring. So I began to strangle on my anger, finding myself unable to sleep and even losing interest in studies that I love. I was unraveling, collapsing inside and coming to realize that if the church was not going to take care of me, I'd have to start taking care of myself. The church is the only army that shoots its wounded, but I refused to let that happen to me. Instead, I fell on my sword."

If honest, every one of us will admit to having faced, and most likely now faces, burnout/stress at unprecedented levels, no matter what one does for work. These days the roles of pastoring are multiple. Pastors, church board members, and we in the pews would do well to read Eugene Peterson's *Working the Angles* and *Underneath the Unpredictable Plant* to be reminded one more time of what true biblical pastoring is about.

In this day it is no secret that helpers need help, in any helping profession. But since this is a book on encouraging pastors, I believe any member of the clergy can avoid this crisis of daily stress and burnout by taking three sincere steps. If persons in your congregation dare to help you, let them. Let them love you, and watch what happens to you both.

STEP ONE: TAKE TIME OFF (REST)

In the March 1984 issue of the Fuller Theological Seminary journal, *Theology, News and Notes*, Dr. Arch Hart introduces the issue of pastoral burnout.

A pattern of emotional overload with little reward or appreciation in the context of feelings of helplessness is at the heart of the burnout syndrome. Why are pastors particularly prone to burnout? Because:

1. They have not been taught to care for others in the right way.
2. They care too much out of guilt.
3. They care too much and feel helpless about providing solutions.
4. They care too much all of the time.
5. They do not care enough about their own self-recovery.

In another article in that same Fuller journal, David Congo reports:

In a national study of ministers from 32 denominations and 38 states . . . the following information was obtained:

1. 85 percent of ministers spent two or less evenings per week at home.
2. 70 percent worked more than 60 hours per week.
3. 61 percent spent less than one hour per week talking with other pastors.
4. 75 percent spent less than one evening per month purely for social time with other couples.
5. 78 percent felt their family freedom was restricted by their career.
6. 40 percent didn't take a regular day off.
7. There were two critical time periods when a pastor was most susceptible to burnout: The first was the first five years in the ministry and the second was after 15 years in the ministry.

What is it in ministry that makes us attempt to do more than even Jesus did? In Luke 5:15 (NIV) we find these words: "Yet the news about him spread all the more, so that crowds of people came to hear him and to be healed of their sicknesses. But Jesus often withdrew to lonely places and prayed."

The Gospels are rampant with indications that our Lord took off periods of time in between His significant days of ministry. Is there an example here to be followed? In our culture? Is what He did not practical anymore? Would He even last as a pastor in one of our modern-day congregations, taking so much time off?

Helping people can be rewarding, but most often it is draining. Athletes expend energy to bring themselves to peak performance, but they punctuate their training with periods of rest that allow the body to reorganize its energy. The athletes getting ready for Olympic competition know that they need to recoup their losses and heal their hurts. Spiritual athletes need to do the same. Spiritual energy needs to be replaced.

Some of the introductory words of Henri Nouwen in his small but powerful book, *In the Name of Jesus: Reflections on Christian Leadership* (pages 9-11), point out how the times of our life can be misused, resulting in burnout:

> After twenty years in the academic world as a teacher of pastoral psychology, pastoral theology and Christian spirituality, I began to experience a deep inner threat. As I entered into my fifties and was able to realize the unlikelihood of doubling my years, I came face to face with the simple question—did becoming older bring me closer to Jesus?
>
> After twenty-five years of priesthood, I found myself praying poorly, living somewhat isolated from other people and very much preoccupied with burning issues. Everyone was saying that I was doing really well. But something inside was telling me that my success was putting my own soul in danger.
>
> I began to ask myself whether my lack of contemplative prayer, my loneliness and my constantly changing involvement in what seemed most urgent were signs that the spirit was gradually being suppressed. It was very hard for me to see clearly. And though I never spoke about hell, or only jokingly so, I woke up one day with the realization that I

was living in a very dark place, and that the term "burnout" was a convenient psychological translation for a spiritual death.

STEP TWO: DEVELOP A CIRCLE OF SAFETY (BE ACCOUNTABLE)

Many pastors who have sought counsel from our ministry to Christian leaders are not closely, carefully, and kindly accountable in their personal lives to a few people of the same sex who will hold their feet to the fire. Those who "hit the wall," burn out, yield to moral failure, or whatever, have avoided a group of caring people who will ask the hard questions.

Church boards may think they are fitting into this role at monthly meetings and annual reviews. But most church boards, from lack of training and input, simply do not know how to care deeply or completely for their pastors. And in many places accountability is looked at as a form of "spiritual police work" instead of as consistently nurturing and caring for the various needs of the pastors at their deepest levels.

This is one place where the meaningful ministry of Promise Keepers applies to the men on both sides of the pulpit. The "Seven Promises of a Promise Keeper," if kept, will encourage maturity in Christ and will help keep pastors accountable in their relationships.

Kevin Perrotta, managing editor of *Faith & Renewal*, wrote in the November/December 1990 issue about "Five Advantages of Pastoral Care for Leaders," used here by permission: This is a solid statement of what correct accountability can do.

1. *Defense Against Temptation*—Temptation, like toadstools, grows in the dark and shrinks in the light. Intimidating temptations appear more manageable when they are brought out of the isolation of our own minds and into the light of another person's faith and love in Christ.
2. *A Help to Purify Motives*—Dutch theologian Jacob Firet points out that leaders' impact on people results not only

from what they consciously intend but also from the atmosphere created by their underlying motivations. He further points out that "the desire to help others in their troubles [may be] interwoven with the desire to shine in the eyes of others." In such cases the pastoral relationship may become twisted to serve the needs of the leader rather than of the person being cared for. Of course, everyone has mixed motivations. The problem is that we usually do not see clearly what the mixture is. We need God to enlighten us. The process, as Firet says, is aided by openness with "competent others."

3. *A Guard Against Self-Deception*—Because they talk constantly about God and His ways, leaders in the church are particularly susceptible to the illusion that they are leading a godly life. They may lose sight of their real selves behind the dazzlement of their own rhetoric. In *Lead Us Not into Temptation*, Don Basham bluntly warns that a pastoral leader who "has not found and submitted himself to some form of personal oversight, which can provide not only encouragement but also correction, is in danger of deception."

4. *Clarify What God Wants Us to Do*—Trusted friends who are able to view our life as a whole can help us sort out which of the many demands on our time God wants us to respond to. One pastor responds to this accountability by saying "it is a protection against doing your own thing. It brings greater confidence that you are doing what God wants you to be doing. You become freer and bolder. If there are difficulties and opposition, you have greater assurance that these are the obstacles God wants you dealing with. Without this, you can easily end up running around doing lots of good things, busy, but haggard and worn out—maybe bearing fruit, maybe not."

5. *Protection Against Burnout*—The factors leading to emotional and spiritual exhaustion have been much studied.

In *Why Christians Burnout*, Charles Perry, Jr., identifies the following as the chief causes:

a. Unrealistic expectations
b. Job infiltration of every part of life
c. Failure to achieve expected advancement
d. Insufficient capacity for the job
e. Low self-esteem
f. Failure after initial success
g. Absence of personal support

No one personal relationship holds the key to any of these problems. But a safe, accountable relationship may help in dealing with all of them. Someone who is close to us and knows us well can help us recognize when we are expecting our work to be more pleasant and satisfying than it is (factor a. above), or when we are taking on work that we do not have the skills to handle (factor d.). This person can point out where we are allowing work to take over our lives (factor b.), and can renew our sense of self-worth (factor e.) when we fail at what we have attempted (factor f.) or when we do not obtain advancement (factor c.). All of this gives the comfort of knowing that someone else really understands and cares (factor g.).

An accountability relationship does not absolutely protect us against burnout or moral failure. There are no non-flammable lives. That is why smoke detector and water sprinkler systems are wise investments.

Additionally, I would encourage you to read chapter 8 of Chuck Swindoll's book *Living Above the Level of Mediocrity* for some solid thinking about accountability. His treatment of the subject is excellent.

STEP THREE: SEEK A MENTOR (TRUST)

In their excellent book *Connecting: The Mentoring Relationships You Need to Succeed in Life*, Paul Stanley and Robert Clinton introduce a frightening thought: few leaders finish well. One of their major premises is, "mentoring can reduce the probability of leadership failure, provide needed accountability, and empower a responsive leader. . . . Mentoring by a spiritual guide, counselor or peer can change lives and ministries." Yet it takes trust of another to seek out mentors in our lives. Even deeper, it takes increased trust of God.

Noted pastor and author Eugene Peterson explains that he sought a spiritual director because "I got scared to death of myself. I saw my capacity for self-deception. Then I looked around and saw colleagues who were just as bad, but weren't doing anything about it. I thought, I've got to do something. I went looking, praying, and searching. In my denominational structure we have administrators, but we don't have bishops to oversee our lives."

I quote further from Stanley and Clinton's *Connecting:*

> The Apostle Paul was obsessed with finishing well. He saw life as a race. When meeting with his beloved Ephesian elders for the last time, he said, "I consider my life worth nothing to me, if only I may finish the race and complete the task the Lord Jesus has given me—the task of testifying to the gospel of God's grace" (Acts 20:24). Paul was so motivated to finish well that he challenged the Corinthian believers to "Run [the race] in such a way as to get the prize. . . . Not . . . running aimlessly" (1 Corinthians 9:24-26). He disciplined his body to make it do what it must, not what it wanted to, so that "[having] preached to others, I myself will not be disqualified for the prize" (verse 27). What joy filled his heart as he testified at the end of his life: "I have fought the good fight. I have finished the race. I have kept the faith" (2 Timothy 4:7).

What moved the apostle Paul to press on, to go all the way? It must have been the same thing that caused Daniel and his three buddies, Shadrach, Meshach, and Abednego, to fix their eyes on God and be His, all the way to the end, no matter what. Or David, Joseph, the apostles, Barnabas, George Mueller, Billy Graham, and thousands of followers of Christ whose names will be known by few, but who have affected those who knew them.

To finish well does not mean to reach perfection, but, like Paul, to keep pressing on toward it. So that when your time comes to an end you are still growing in your love for Christ and in intimacy with Him, still pressing on to make Him known, still living as His disciple and loving the people God places in your life, and relentlessly seeking to know and do God's will.

What are the characteristics of those who finish well, according to the research of Stanley and Clinton?

1. They had *perspective* that enabled them to focus.
2. They enjoyed *intimacy with Christ* and experienced repeated times of *inner renewal*.
3. They were *disciplined* in important areas of life.
4. They maintained a *positive learning attitude* all their lives.
5. They had a network of *meaningful relationships* and several important *mentors* during their lifetime.

There is no magical potion for reducing daily stress and the threat of burnout, no sure formula, no one way it can be done. So much more needs to be said about this issue. You, and those you sincerely and humbly allow into your life to care for you, will add individual, significant ideas to dealing with daily stress and burnout. But I trust that this has stirred you up and stimulated your creativity for what is to come.

To all care-givers, I hope that before you step out to help another you will consider for yourself these same three steps:

1. Take time off (*rest*).
2. Develop a circle of safety (*be accountable*).
3. Seek a mentor (*trust*).

WHO CAN HELP US CARE FOR OUR PASTORS?

A headline in the July 21, 1995, *St. Louis Post-Dispatch* read, "Clayton Minister Commits Suicide."

What do we do with that one? Earlier on that day through a telephone call I had already heard about this tragedy. The young man who took his life was the younger brother of our former pastor here in Denver. Even though I did not know this person well, I know other members of the family fairly well. As I write this my heart grieves for and with them. I sit here shaking my head in disbelief.

But no matter what I may be feeling at a distance, I cannot even begin to imagine what my former pastor is feeling or thinking — or his family, or the widow and children of this man who is no more, or the members and friends of this good church in a fine St. Louis suburb. As newspaper articles were faxed to me from St. Louis, I found myself with my own wide range of emotions — helpless, angry, sad, stunned, curious. These emotions have only fueled my resolve to see Christian leaders strengthened in all their relationships — with God, with themselves, with their families, friends, and coworkers — and to finish this book so that *together* we can be of better support and encouragement to our pastors.

The truth remains: We can do everything right, with all the right motives, and it may not be enough. We can give all the care and concern in the world, and it still comes down to whether it will be received or not.

However, *let us make a strong resolve to do all we can!*

This promising young man on the pastoral horizon was an all-out, 100-percent kind of guy. Though there had been some personal and family difficulties in his youth, he had seemed to be one of the overcomers. By all visible appearances, he seemed to have had a special anointing from God for pastoral ministry.

In his young adult life he had recovered from a serious mountain-climbing fall. His brother had been taken by leukemia, and his dad had died while he was in college. He lived with the hard fact and ache that two of his three children were not normal. He was back in the pulpit after living through a train accident that caused the amputation of one of his legs in the spring of 1995. He was thirty-six, bright, articulate, with a doctorate from a leading seminary, the pastor of one of the largest evangelical congregations in our country.

If you were to know more of this man's story, you could second-guess what happened until you were out of breath. From our human perspectives we can say, "What a useless tragedy." But this awful happening only serves to underscore that no one can fully know what is going on in the heart and mind of another. Only our God knows that.

The newspaper articles I've been sent indicate that people were hanging in there with this man to the extent he allowed them in. Read thoughtfully the letter he sent to his congregation as reprinted in the *St. Louis Post-Dispatch* of Saturday, July 22, 1995 used here by permission.

> These are some of the most strange and difficult words that I have ever attempted to write. How I came to be in this emotional state, I honestly do not know. Ever since the accident, it seems that I've been fighting a losing battle with depression and despair. I write this letter, neither to justify my behavior nor to make anyone feel guilty for what has happened, but rather to apologize to our entire church. I know of nothing which any of you could have done to change my situation. Out of the countless sins that I have committed in this life, it is my own wretched weakness for which I am most ashamed.
>
> In the history of this great church, my office has been held by many fine and godly men. I am deeply ashamed to know that I am the first one to fail it so miserably. I assure you, however, that this was never my intention. It seems that I am having some sort of "nervous breakdown," and it is a terrifying feeling. Some of you even tried to warn me about the folly of trying to do too much, too soon (God bless those of you who did). But the truth of the matter is, once I had jumped back in "full steam," it seemed that there was just no slowing down.

God forgive me for not being any stronger than I am. But when a minister becomes clinically depressed, there are very few places where he can turn for help (at least not without ruining his ministry). I did try to seek help where I could. I even went to see a local psychiatrist. Though not a believer, he is a fine man. He put me on Prozac; then he doubled the dosage; and still it feels as if I'm sinking farther and farther into a downward spiral of depression. I feel like a drowning man, trying frantically to lift up my head to take just one more breath. But one way or the other, I know that I am going down.

Forgive me for being such an unfaithful shepherd. But never doubt that God's Word remains true, even if the messenger is fallen. Upon that one hope, I have staked my entire life. Whatever desperate or foolish things I have done, it does not (and cannot) nullify the Word of God. I would implore you, as the spiritual leaders of our church, to remind our members of that great truth in this time of crisis. I would also beg you not to shun my family because of my own selfish deeds. I am even more terrified for them at this moment than I am for myself. I have no right to ask this (or anything else) of you, but I would urge you, gentlemen, to recognize that my family needs your help *now* more than ever before.

May God have mercy upon my soul for the damage which I have caused to His church, His name and — worst of all — to my own beloved family. It has always been true, but now, more than ever, I know that my only hope is in the blood of Christ.

Yours in the Name of Our Blessed Lord,
Our Only Hope in Life and Death
— Tim Brewer

That this is sobering is an understatement. It was *never* my intention to begin and end this book with the stories of the seemingly senseless and untimely deaths of two pastors. These are the extreme realities of life.

But, thank God, there is help, assistance, and encouragement out there! Please read on.

EXTRA HELP AND CARE IS AVAILABLE FOR YOUR PASTOR—AND YOU

There will be times in your developing relationship with your pastor when that thoughtful note, gift, or specific action of love and care will not be enough. You may begin to sense that something is not quite right, and you can't put your finger on what it is.

Again, check your motives here, and with enough personal prayer to back you up, follow your discernment. Share your concerns, whatever they are, with your pastor first. Then, if necessary, be willing to go with your pastor to the chairman of your church board and offer to be the right conduit of grace, love, and care for whatever the needs may be.

If you are on target with the correct motives of your own heart, your pastor will move one of several directions. He may weep or sigh with relief at his needs finally being recognized. Many pastors find it hard to be open and honest with their needs. There is a myth that pastors are supposed to be perfect—no problems, no needs. But that only goes for dead pastors. The really good, growing pastors I know are the ones who can admit they are needy and then are willing to seek and/or take the care and encouragement that is available.

You may also find your pastor moving into "hyper-caution" when you extend some honest friendship and concern. Strange but true, many Bible colleges and seminaries, and a lot of "old-time" pastors, directly and indirectly warn their students and associate staff to be careful about having close friends within their congregations—"You know, you just can't trust people these days." In my opinion, that myth comes straight out of "the pit." I cannot deny that so many in ministry are poorly treated, some in ways you would find hard to believe. But if ministry is not about relationships, what is it about?

You may also find your pastor moving into a defensive mode. It may seem to him that you are saying, "Pastor, you are not able to take care of yourself in this area of your life. I will help you" (who among us likes to have our lack of competence and sins pointed out?). When all you are really saying is, "Pastor, I'd like to be more of a friend to you than I've been. I'm not asking to be your best friend—that is up to you—but I long to be a better friend and member of this body of believers."

You could also be dead wrong in whatever you think you are discerning. Admit that, if you are. But what if you are right? What if you are in the ball park? What if that gut reaction of yours stays, even after much prayer? What do you do then?

Your pastor could be living and moving in denial. Careful, you could be too. Denial is a unique mechanism of the mind that is often fueled by a troubled and restless heart. I've never met a drunk yet who didn't claim to be able to walk a straight line.

Many wasted, burned-out, depressed pastors will outwardly deny they are living in denial, and yet when they wake up in the morning they do not know where they will get the energy they need to face the day. They really want to run and hide. But what do they do? Oh, they try working harder, filling up more of their schedule, refusing to take time out to relax and play and to be quiet, and spending even less time with their spouse and family.

Relief, at the extreme, at any cost, becomes their subtle, insidious goal, their antidote to denial. That often gets played out in immoral, illegal, and unethical ways, or in hyperactivity, or in disappearing from the responsibility of their duties, at first only in their mind, their thoughts, and then in their actions, their responses to life. Denial is one of the major diseases of fallen leaders, or those who will fall someday.

Shouldn't they know better? we ask.

Of course. And they do. Just like you and I do when we sin our own sins and then try to justify and/or deny our own way through life. Pastors are people. You are too. But that lets none of us off the hook.

So where does one turn when the encouragement creatively and genuinely offered is not enough? What are my choices when I really do have a genuine care for my pastor?

A number of ministries have come into existence in recent years to help encourage and strengthen Christian leaders. Our own ministry, Life Enrichment, is a source of referral of care and encouragement for pastors, missionaries, parachurch workers, and other leaders in the marketplace.

WHO DOES CARE FOR PASTORS AND OTHER CHRISTIAN LEADERS?

Since the late 1980s I've become increasingly aware of a growing group of dedicated individuals who have a tremendous heart for clergy and other Christian leaders. What follows is a listing of a number of places that give extra care to these people. The services of these ministries range from significant in-depth therapy, to week-long renewal programs, to a combination of counseling and consulting, to places of rest and refreshment in a bed and breakfast environment.

Many of these people I know personally, but not all. A few I count as extra close partners in ministry. It is my privilege to maintain this listing for both *Leadership Journal* and the division of Church Relations for Promise Keepers. This listing is available for other groups and publications on a "permission-granted" basis. Please write to me for more details before reproducing this list in any form.

I also welcome your help in getting this list out to as many people as possible through the distribution of this important and timely book. As other acceptable, qualified, well-proven ministries become known, they will be added to this list. You may want to write to me for new additions. Look under Life Enrichment in the following list to get my address.

These ministries have proven to be helpful to pastors and their spouses, their churches and denominational structures, as well as missionaries and other Christian leaders. You will find places and people throughout North America, the United Kingdom, New Zealand, and Australia who have a deep heart for encouraging Christian leaders.

The services of these ministries varies, as do their costs. Their commitment to helping your pastor get to the right place or person for healing, wholeness, and restoration is unswerving.

I thank God for these people and their commitment to extend dynamic care to a wide variety of Christian leaders, especially pastors. They are ready to serve you and those you care about, in whatever way possible.

We are in this together, to support our local pastors.

≈

Ashram of the Almighty
Pastor Bob and Phyllis Heneghan
P.O. Box 1196
Buena Vista, CO 81211
719/395-6881

Ashram is a word originally from India, meaning hermitage or a retreat for making disciples. Our Lord found it essential as part of His disciples' training to spend countryside and mountain time apart (Mark 9:2, John 3:22). This is a place where pastors can get in touch with themselves and learn how to be alone with God in the quiet, to find strength and heart enlargement for personal integrity and ministry empowerment. This is accomplished through contemplative prayer and worship.

Barnabas Ministries
Pastors Dick and Dee Sochacki
39391 Roslyn Drive
Sterling Heights, MI 48313
810/264-6638

Barnabas Ministries offers encouragement to hurting, wounded, discharged, burned-out, sinning, and happy pastors and wives and church leaders. Their focus is the independent and non-denominational ministries. They are also a resource for ministries available to pastors, wives, etc.; everything from counseling to places of retreat, and anything in between.

Called Together Ministries
Linda Riley, Director
20820 Avis Avenue
Torrance, CA 90503
310/793-9747
FAX: 310/539-0007
Listening Line — 800/378-4370

Called Together Ministries has a significant and needed focus on pastors' wives and women in ministry. This group offers an extensive mail-order resource catalog, a "Listening Line" for telephone peer counseling, referral services, a free newsletter, retreats, and seminars.

Center for Continuing Education at the Episcopal Theological Seminary in Virginia
Richard Busch, Ph.D., Director
3737 Seminary Road
Alexandria, VA 22304
703/370-6600
FAX: 703/370-6234

Their six-week renewal and growth programs provide a unique opportunity for ecumenical clergy to come away from the pressures of ministry. The appeal of this group is to pastors seeking to discover new ways to face the challenges of ministry; deepen their relationship with Jesus Christ so as to enrich and revitalize their life and ministry; gain a greater sense of personal integration and balance; discern what God may be calling them to be and do; and increase their effectiveness to serve the local congregation.

Christian Prayer Retreat House
George and Jan Bauer
8810 State Highway 103
Idaho Springs, CO 80452
303/567-4601

This beautiful, quiet setting beside a cascading mountain stream, an hour west of Denver, is designed to offer a place of encounter between God and persons serving Him, to provide opportunities to nourish their spiritual growth, to support and equip persons for more vital, creative, and joyful service, whatever their ministry may be. Here each retreatant will be immersed in extended times of prayer and companionship devoted to knowing God better, while surrounded by the splendors of nature. Accommodations are available for overnight stays of several days' duration as well as day visits, with meals included.

Church Health
Richard L. Bergstrom, D.Min.
P.O. Box 2112
Bellingham, WA 98227
360/676-4824
FAX: 360/676-0748
E-mail: Church Dr@aol.com
Church Health works with pastors and churches to promote healthy leaders and congregations. This ministry offers coaching to pastors in a mentoring relationship through formal leadership networks within geographical areas. The members of this team go on site to consult churches in the midst of conflict and crisis, and to facilitate revitalization and growth.

The Claybury Trust
Colin Buckland, Executive Director
266 Camrose Avenue
Edgware, Middlesex HA8 6AG
United Kingdom
081/952-1064
FAX: 081/381-2124
E-mail: CompuServe — 100337,3220
The Claybury Trust exists to serve the church of Jesus Christ in the United Kingdom (England, Scotland, Wales, and Ireland) and throughout Europe by offering encouragement, healing, and resources that are designed to positively benefit pastors, missionaries, and other Christian leaders in their own lives and in all other relationships. Training, counseling, consulting, and audio/video and printed resources are available. The Trust seeks to keep a list of places of rest, refreshment, and renewal. These programs function effectively across interdenominational lines.

CORE Resources
Kenneth D. Cope, M.A.
P.O. Box 175
White House, TN 37188
615/783-1744
E-mail: CompuServe — 74462,2660
CORE Resources works with Christian leaders individually, in their marriages, through personal career assessment, and in organizational team building. With a network of associates, this group offers workshops on relationships, career assessment and leadership

development. CORE Resources exists to Cultivate Occupational/ Organizational and Relational Effectiveness by dealing with core issues that promote growth and development in the individual, couple, team, organization, and community.

Eagle's Nest Retreat Ministries
Rev. John Gowins, Ph.D.
P.O. Box 437
Ouray, CO 81427
800/533-4049

Eagle's Nest is designed specifically for ministers and their families. It offers professional counseling for those in need of support and guidance. Eagle's Nest also offers vacation times at minimal cost. John and his wife, Kay, have been involved in pastoral ministry and counseling for over twenty-five years. Ouray is located in the beautiful San Juan Mountains of southern Colorado and provides a perfect setting for rest and restoration.

Eagle's Rest
Stan and Liz Carlson
N701 Park Drive
Ogema, WI 54459
715/767-5445

This is a retreat ministry to pastoral and missionary couples in a beautiful northwoods lake setting. Recreational activities include hiking, boating, fishing, cross-country and downhill skiing, golf, and nearby scenic trips, all in country settings. You will find this a perfect place for rest, renewal, and encouragement. Counseling is optional. Their desire is to be there for ministry couples when needed, no matter the reason or the circumstances.

Fairhaven Ministries
Charles Shepson, Director
Route 2, Box 1022
Roan Mountain, TN 37687
615/772-4269

Fairhaven was established to be a safe place to which Christian leaders could come for counseling, or just for rest and relaxation, where qualified counselors would be available upon request to meet with them. Pastors and missionaries from all over the world are received and helped, no matter what their affiliation may be. Facilities are deliberately first class as a part of the healing atmosphere.

Focus on the Family — Pastoral Ministries Department

Rev. H. B. London, Jr., Rev. Dan Davidson, Rev. Roger Charman,
Stan Kellner, Robert Waliszewski
8605 Explorer Drive
Colorado Springs, CO 80920
719/531-3360
FAX: 719/531-3347

Rev. H. B. London, Jr., heads up Focus on the Family's efforts
to support pastors and their families through resources, referrals,
and personal consultation. Resources include a bimonthly audiocas-
sette series called *Pastor to Pastor*, a weekly fax newsletter called
The Pastor's Weekly Briefing, economical *Family Resource
Libraries* for nonprofit ministries, plus several booklets geared
toward pastors, their families, and their congregations. Regional
pastor gatherings are scheduled year-round to provide opportunities
for fellowship and encouragement among pastors and spouses.
Clergy Appreciation Month is promoted each October, encouraging
congregations to recognize and honor their pastors for their spiritual
leadership.

Fulfillment in Ministry — For Christian Ministers and Laity

Ed Bratcher, Director
3912 Sturbridge Drive
Durham, NC 27713
919/490-4807

Fulfillment in Ministry focuses on identifying the hazards, the
tools, and the rewards of parish ministry. This is carried out through
lectures, retreats, writing, and counseling.

Gray Fox Ranch

Walter and Francoise Becker, Directors
P.O. Box 434
Alto, NM 88312
800/336-4405
FAX: 505/336-9126

Gray Fox Ranch is a marital retreat for ministers and spouses
in a year-round mountain resort area. Only one couple at a time
spends a week at the ranch for counseling on personal, marital, and
vocational concerns in daily, individual, and couple sessions. The
Beckers, married thirty years and licensed therapists, provide pri-

vate accommodations, meals, and hours of unscheduled time for refreshment and renewal.

Idaho Mountain Ministries
David and Carolyn Roper
2503 Bruins Circle
Boise, ID 83704
208/376-6607
FAX: 208/376-2633
E-mail: CompuServe—71222,2121

Idaho Mountain Ministries (IMM) exists to serve as a resource to pastoral couples in Idaho and beyond. The primary focus is on those ministering in smaller churches and/or rural locations. IMM is dedicated to standing with these men and women to encourage and support them through regional pastors' conferences, special ministries to pastors' wives, pulpit supply, telephone support, personal counseling, support and study groups for reflection, prayer, and mutual growth in one's personal life and ministry.

Institute of Biblical Leadership
Dr. Russell F. Lloyd, Founder and President
2466 South Old Oaks Drive
Beavercreek, OH 45431
Phone/FAX: 513/429-2700

The Institute of Biblical Leadership (IBL) is a ministry of encouragement to the leadership of the church worldwide. Pastors, lay leaders, missionaries, parachurch leaders, churches, and missions receive the ministry in one or a combination of several areas: (1) Leadership Teaching—on biblical principles of leadership; (2) Preaching/Speaking—on issues of leadership; (3) Biblical Counseling—with practical application of God's Word; (4) Organizational Consultation—on a full range of issues supporting organizational effectiveness; (5) Crisis Response—on site, for all parties involved. A complimentary video is available by request. There are plans in the future to move this ministry to Lake Lure, North Carolina. If you discover the above address and phone number are invalid, check with Lake Lure directory assistance.

John Mark Ministries
Rev. Dr. Rowland Croucher
7 Bangor Court
Heathmont
Australia 3135
Phone/FAX: (03)729-2517

Rev. Les Scarborough
23 Alam Street
St. Marys, Australia 2760
Phone/FAX: (02)623-4813

This is a unique ministry formed to pioneer cross-denominational research relating to ex-clergy; establish ministry-support structures for pastors; provide consultative expertise to denominations in the selection, training, formation, continuing education, and care of their ministers; and above all, to provide encouragement to churches to be loving, healthy, and effective communities of faith. This is all accomplished through leadership enhancement, supporting and encouraging ex-pastors, consulting, counseling, seminars and motivational talks, pastor-renewal retreats, mentoring and equipping, and small-group training.

Kettering Clergy Care Center
Robert Peach, D.Min., LPCC, Director
1259 East Dorothy Lane
Kettering, OH 45419
513/299-5288 or 800/324-8618
FAX: 513/296-4276
E-mail: CompuServe — 74617,2613

This center offers professional care and support to ministers, missionaries, leaders, and employees of church organizations and their families. Services available are counseling, crisis intervention weekends, two-week individual and couple counseling, clergy burnout prevention, clergy marriage enrichment, instruction for boards of congregations, premarital and marital assessment programs. The Ministry Care Line is also available, which is a national subscription phone consultation and support program for church professionals.

Lake Martin Marriage Retreat
Forrest and Nancy Mobley, Directors
1677 Andrews Mill Road
Tallassee, AL 36078
334/857-2165
FAX: 334/857-2365
E-mail: CompuServe — 72203,533

Designed to refresh and renew marriages, Lake Martin teaches and counsels through individualized programs. Four to six couples gather for group teaching, fellowship, and meals. The Mobleys draw on their experience of thirty-two years of marriage, of counseling many couples, and in God's healing of their own marriage.

The Leadership Center
Rev. David B. Morgan, Director
31 Old Lakeview Terrace
Wolfboro, NH 03809
603/569-8607 or 603/569-3922

This ministry is dedicated to serving New England church leaders. The Leadership Center, using excellent accommodations on beautiful Lake Winnipesaukee, offers time to think, study and plan; time for physical relaxation and refreshment; time for interaction with men and women of wisdom and experience; time for warm Christian fellowship with those of like mind. The Leadership Center is interdenominational, costs are reasonable because of contributions, and programs are offered year round.

Life Enrichment
Wes Roberts, President
14581 East Tufts Avenue
Denver/Aurora, CO 80015
303/693-3954
FAX: 303/766-9134
E-mail: CompuServe — 103006,3320

Curt Anderson, Director of Counseling
222 West 2nd Avenue
Plainwell, MI 49080
616/685-2244
E-mail: CompuServe — 74031,14

Since 1982 Life Enrichment has existed to see Christian leaders worldwide (pastors, missionaries, parachurch workers, and those in the marketplace) strengthened in all their relationships at home, in their lifework/ministry, and in their leisure. This is accomplished through (1) consulting with the senior leader, his board, and his staff to strengthen working relationships and clarify vision; (2) spiritual direction, biblical counseling, and professional therapy for the wounded, hurting leader, his spouse, his family, and his immediate work/ministry team; and (3) through the provision of places and programs of brief intensive counseling and rest, renewal, and refreshment for leaders throughout North America, England, and Europe.

Link Care Center
Ken Royer, D.Min, or Brent Lindquist, Ph.D.
1734 West Shaw Avenue
Fresno, CA 93711
209/439-5920
FAX: 209/439-2214
E-mail: CompuServe — 75027,2265
Link Care Center provides comprehensive counseling services to people in ministry and missions around the world. The programs are tailor-made to the participant and vary from one week to several months, or longer. The staff includes psychologists, psychiatrists, marriage and family counselors, pastoral care, and language and cultural consultants. They work with individuals, couples, and families. They typically have twenty to twenty-five families in residence at any one time in studios, one- or three-bedroom apartments. Many fees can be covered by insurance. Link Care also offers a wide variety of consultation, education, and training services for missionaries, ministers, missions, churches, and organizational administrators.

Makahiki Ministries
Bruce Fincham, Executive Director
Lana Luczy, Director of Hospitality Homes International Network
P.O. Box 415
Mariposa, CA 95338
Phone/FAX: 209/966-2988
Makahiki Ministries helps Christian leaders find places for rest and renewal. Named for an old Hawaiian festival of peace and rest, this ministry offers a network of hospitality homes in the United States and several foreign countries for Christian workers seeking spiritual and physical renewal. Counseling referrals are available.

Newsletters and seminars are also offered covering biblical views of stress and Christian hospitality.

Marble Retreat
Louis and Melissa McBurney
139 Bannockburn
Marble, CO 81623
970/963-2499
E-mail: CompuServe—72040,1327

This retreat is an interdenominational crisis-counseling center designed to meet the needs of Christian ministers and their spouses. Up to four couples come for two weeks of individual and group counseling. Located high in the central Rockies, Marble Retreat offers each couple their own private accommodations with meals shared family style. The atmosphere at eight thousand feet above sea level is low on oxygen, but high on acceptance, warmth, and love. It is a place where healing begins.

Marriage and Family Enrichment
David and Linda Marriott
69 Nigel Road
Browns Bay, Auckland 10
New Zealand
Phone/FAX: (09) 4797275

This ministry is for the purpose of producing strong, healthy, and enriched marriage and family relationships for pastors, for church leaders, and within the churches and communities of New Zealand. A living, personal relationship with Jesus Christ, more than twenty-six years of marriage, twenty-two years of pastoral ministry, six children, and many of the joys, struggles, and pains of life have equipped these leaders for this ministry.

Ministers Counseling Service, BGCT
Glenn Booth, Director
4144 North Central Expressway, Suite 1160
Dallas, TX 75204
214/826-6591

This is a ministry to all ministers and their families who serve in a Texas Baptist Church or an agency of the Baptist General Convention of Texas. The services include counseling, referrals to other counselors, counseling subsidies, conferences, workshops, seminars, and retreats.

Ministers Network
Bill Schraven, Executive Director
504 Lake Street
Beaver Dam, WI 53916
414/887-7850
FAX: 414/887-7850 *51
E-mail: PinnacleMn@aol.com

The mission of this division of Pinnacle Ministries is to be available to ministers for the express purpose of encouraging and equipping quality leaders to greater effectiveness in ministry as a lifelong vocation. This nondenominational organization is dedicated to ministering to full-time Christian workers (pastors, parachurch leaders, and missionaries) through the provision of superior retreat facilities, conference speakers, training seminars, consulting services, and referrals. All staff are involved in local church ministries and understand the needs for and challenges to ministry. This group holds to the philosophy that ministry was never meant to be a solo act. They are there for you when you need to add to your resource team.

Ministries Resource Center
Rev. Gerald and Alita Robertson, M.S., Co-founders
14190 Barker Hollow Road
Woodman, WI 53827
608/988-4649

Located on fifty-three acres in a scenic hollow near the Wisconsin and Mississippi Rivers, Ministries Resource Center offers a furnished home available for rest, recreation, spiritual renewal, or on-site counseling. Services include individual or group counseling, crisis counseling and intervention, and marriage and family counseling. Seminars are also provided as requested in conflict management, pastor/board relationships, and marriage enrichment. Gerald has extensive pastoral experience and Alita is a Wisconsin state-certified marriage and family therapist.

Mountain Top Retreat
Harold and Beulah Erickson
13705 Cottonwood Canyon Drive
Bozeman, MT 59715
406/763-4566

This is a ministry of encouragement to ministers and missionaries who wish to find a quiet place for rest and renewal. Individual

modern guest houses provide privacy in a beautiful mountain setting. Personnel are available to any who wish to share their
burdens.

Paraklesis Ministries
Dr. Sidney Draayer, Director
1550 East Beltline SE, Suite 340
Grand Rapids, MI 49506
616/458-6759 or 800/421-8352
FAX: 616/957-1699
E-mail: CompuServe—75721,232

The purpose of Paraklesis Ministries is to provide personal
encouragement and support to pastors, missionaries, and their
spouses. They seek to fulfill that purpose through promoting a
healthful lifestyle defined as spiritual vitality, physical wellness,
emotional maturity, and harmonious relationships. The program
includes five-day retreats, counseling, seminars, and support
groups. They provide training for church staffs as well as testing for
ministerial candidates. Speakers for retreats are also available.

Pine Rest Christian Mental Health Services
Ken Ellis, Ph.D., Coordinator, Christian Ministry Service
300 - 68th Street SE
Grand Rapids, MI 49501
616/455-5000, ext. 2952
E-mail: CompuServe—70651,1625

The Christian Ministry Service is a specialty program designed
to meet the needs of pastors, missionaries, parachurch workers, and
Christian school teachers, as well as their spouses and children.
Consultation, counseling, and psychiatric interventions for a wide
range of stress, marital, and mental health problems are offered
both on and off campus by trained professionals in psychiatry, psychology, social work, and chaplaincy.

Resources for Resolving Conflict, Inc.
Marlin E. Thomas, D.Min., President
2123 Wold Avenue
P.O. Box 9673
Colorado Springs, CO 80932
719/380-1065
FAX: 719/574-7885
E-mail: methomas@aol.com

Resources for Resolving Conflict, Inc. exists to assist churches and ministry organizations in resisting the destructive effects of internal conflict, abuse that renders ministry and service ineffective. This mission is accomplished through the efforts of prayer, biblical education and training, consultation, mediation, counseling, guidance, and publication. Consultants will travel on location, or consult by fax, telephone, or e-mail. They will provide long-term guidance for churches and ministries in serious difficulty, and will present weekend retreats and training events for those who wish to learn how to avoid the negative consequences of conflict.

Restoration Ministry
Dixon Murrah, M.A., L.M.F.T.
11514 Hughes Road
Houston, TX 77089
713/484-7426
FAX: 713/484-9396
E-mail: drfreud2@aol.com

This ministry offers professional counseling for ministers and their families at no cost. One of the primary activities is a week-long "Stress in the Ministry" conference for minister and spouse. This conference deals with the real issues and is not the normal stress-management approach. It provides a time of renewal, refreshment, and restoration, and it is preventive as well as therapeutic. The conferences are offered five times during the year as a ministry of Sagemont Church in Houston.

Shepherd's Care
Steve and Jeannie Harper, Directors
1910 Harrodsburg Road, Suite 201
Lexington, KY 40503
606/275-5054
FAX: 606/275-1932
E-mail: shepcare@aol.com

Shepherd's Care "ministry to ministers" exists to enrich the joy, fulfillment, and spiritual vitality of clergy and spouses. It offers a variety of ministries: seminars and retreats, spiritual direction, nonprofessional counseling, audiocassettes, referral service, telephone contact, consultation with congregations and leaders on clergy-care issues, and Shepherd's Care OnLine—a subscription-based e-mail newsletter.

Solitary Ministries
Rev. Rick and Barb Floyd
P.O. Box 88005
Grand Rapids, MI 48518
616/667-1948 or 616/457-0132

Solitary Ministries offers a critical care plan for Christian leaders and churches. The purpose is to aid in their vitality, vision, and viability. Their multitract programs include: Tract 1—nondirected guests (day-weekend packages); Tract 2—semidirected guests (three-day packages); Tract 3—directed guests (eight-day packages). All of these packages will allow ample rest time within the beauty of God's creation. Rev. Floyd is available for speaking engagements, seminars, conferences, association meetings, etc. Primary target groups are independent, fundamental Christian leaders and associations in the Great Lakes states. Resources include: *Solitary Moments*—prayer guide; *Solitary Minutes*—quarterly newsletter; *Solitary Messages*—encouraging tapes.

SonScape Ministries
Bob and Sandy Sewell, Directors
P.O. Box 7777
Woodland Park, CO 80866
719/687-7007

This is a place of rest, privacy, creative input, and intimacy in the shadow of Pikes Peak, just outside Colorado Springs in Woodland Park. SonScape is a spiritual retreat, a place of *Vacare Deo*, emptying oneself before the Lord for His refilling. It is here one can take time for personal sharing and counsel about the "red flag" areas of ministry and form strategies to alleviate these stresses. SonScape is preventive maintenance.

Southwest Counseling Associates
Rev. Gary J. Oliver, Ph.D., Clinical Director
Rev. Daniel W. Trathen, D.Min., Ph.D., Program and Training Director
141 West Davies Avenue
Littleton, CO 80120
303/730-1717
FAX: 303/730-1531
E-mail: CompuServe — 75402,3427

Southwest Counseling Associates (SCA) specializes in working with Christian leaders (pastors, missionaries, parachurch workers) in Colorado or on-site anywhere in the world. Through the PastorCare and Missionary Care Services (MCS) ministries, the SCA staff provides candidate and wellness assessments, intensive solution-focused reentry, and crisis counseling for the individual, couple, and family as well as consultation and training. Both PastorCare and MCS have transportation, lodging, and medical services available at no cost or at reduced rates. Many treatment services may be covered by insurance.

Stonegate Resources
Dr. Harry W. Schaumburg
3055 Woodview Court
Colorado Springs, CO 80918
719/548-0908
FAX: 719/548-0739
E-mail: CompuServe — 74361,3050

Stonegate Resources offers brief intensive counseling to Christian leaders. Sessions of individual/couple counseling are held for five to ten days in a retreat setting. Dr. Schaumburg is a nationally recognized counselor specializing in sexual issues. In addition to counseling, seminars and radio programs are given throughout the country on the topic of "False Intimacy: Barrier to Developing Sexual Character."

Synergia
Greg and Meryem Brown
78 Margaret Street
Toowoomba, Queensland 4350
Australia
076-32-0911 or 076-38-1070

Confidential counseling service (donation only) to ministers and manse families. Facilitation of workshops on clergy-care issues (for example, conflict management, stress management, marriage enrichment, sexual temptation, counseling micro skills). Consultants to churches regarding strategic planning and mediation are also available.

Triple Creek Ranch in Illinois and Rancho Mira Sol in Colorado
Jim and Ginny Neece
348 N. Snipe Hollow Road
Elizabeth, IL 61028
815/858-2435

The purpose of these two ranches is to provide facilities for physical and spiritual refreshment and rest to evangelical, full-time Christian pastors and missionaries and their families. The 700-acre Illinois ranch is in the northwest corner of the state near Galena. The 1,300-acre Colorado ranch is in the southwest corner of the state near Durango. Both ranches are situated near historic towns and include completely furnished guest houses, wildlife viewing, hiking, sightseeing, fishing, domestic animals, expansive views, and plenty of quiet.

Tuscarora Resource Center
Lewis A. Judy, Ed.D., Executive Director
870 Sunrise Boulevard
Mt. Bethel, PA 18343
717/897-5115
FAX: 717/897-0144

The Center provides restorative (counseling) and preventive (education, team building, retreats, consultations, assessments) programming to pastors and missionaries and to their organizations. Most of the work is short-term counseling done with people living in residence at the retreat center in the Poconos, but services are also provided worldwide. Their counseling approach is tailor-made to the needs of the individual, couple, or family. The staff provides a combination of pastoral and psychological care with a biblically based approach.

~

Being on this list does not imply acceptance or nonacceptance of the care-giving, counseling, or consulting methods used by each group. We are simply letting you know of ministries that have a heart for Christian leaders. Contacting these groups is entirely voluntary with no responsibility being taken by *Leadership Journal*, Life Enrichment, NavPress, or Wes Roberts for actions taken by anyone representing any group or individuals on this list.

IF YOU WANT TO ADD TO THE LIST

If you are familiar with other good places and people who specifically offer care to pastors, missionaries, and other Christian leaders, please let the author, Wes Roberts, know. You may write to him at the address listed for Life Enrichment in Colorado. Please send the name of the leading person, ministry name, address, and daytime phone number so that the potential of adding them to this list might be explored. Thank you.

EPILOGUE

Thank you for journeying through these pages with me. It is my earnest prayer that you will have both some great fun and sincere pondering as you work hard and creatively at supporting your local pastor and family. May God bless you for every effort you put forth. I would count it a privilege if you would let me know what has worked well in supporting your pastor, so that other pastors and congregations can be encouraged too. Let's be committed to spreading the joy around!

In conclusion, I encourage you to read the following letter. It was first published in the Winter 1992 edition of our ministry newsletter, *Catch Up on Life*, and was written from the perspective of the beginning of a new year. The message rings loud and clear for all time. You have my permission to pass it along to a Christian leader for whom you have a deep, abiding care and concern.

AN OPEN LETTER TO EVERY CHRISTIAN LEADER
ALIVE TODAY

Dear Christian Leader,

Whoever you are, whether easily recognized or known by only a few, whether talented or fledgling. Age doesn't matter. Wherever you are, whether rural or small town, in a suburban setting, big city, or inner city, or even international. Whatever you do, be it church work, missions, parachurch, business, or professional.

Looking back over this past year, in some ways it could be called a very good year. There were moments of joy. And in some ways it was not good. There were moments of pain. What will the year to come be for you?

If you're the "above average" Christian leader, you have some hopes, some dreams, some plans for what you would like to accomplish in the months to come. The lessons learned from last year, and previous years, have made you wiser in some measure.

If life didn't go exactly the way you'd hoped last year, both personally and in your lifework, you have probably determined to work harder this year. Goals not fulfilled last year have either been forgotten or replaced, or your efforts will be doubled to make them succeed in the days to come.

If you experienced any disappointments in relationships last year, no matter how small or large, in your marriage, at home with your family, in your work, with your friends, you probably have a little more cautious attitude this year. The good moments you did experience you possibly look at with some degree of envy, hoping for some form of duplication again this year, if you can find the strength and determination "to do it all right."

One famous author of the 1980s was correct when he began his best-selling book with the single sentence, "Life is difficult." If you and I can be gut-grinding honest, when we face difficult, painful moments, we want relief — soon, now, fast, today. We have been trained from birth to pacify ourselves when life hurts or is uncomfortable, when we don't get what we want. Relief has become big business in our culture, even in our Christian subculture.

Looking back at last year, it has been my privilege to know about some mighty courageous people, all people you and I would put into the category of "Christian leader." Among them have been:

▶ The pastor's wife who went into several months of treatment for her drug addiction, which she kept covered for years. (Secrets rarely remain secrets if they stay unaddressed.)

► The business executive who has served actively on church and parachurch boards and who admitted to his sexual addiction of visiting prostitutes while traveling, while ignoring his wife and family when in town because of "all that needed to be done" in his Christian spheres of influence. (Honest repentance here is bringing healing to many relationships.)

► The winsome, rising "star" of a particular church group who *did not* accept the call to pastor the larger, more prestigious church knowing it would be a type of death to his "career path" by incurring the "wrath" of the denominational hierarchy, but it would be life to his marriage and family life (and thus to his children's children and to those saints he is now serving in his "smaller" place of service).

► The youth pastor who, with fear and trembling, shared his tendency for homosexual desires and fantasies, and was dangerously close to going over the line in a relationship. (You wouldn't know this from how he ministered, looked, walked, talked, played sports, or interacted with females.)

► The professional athlete who confessed to some seriously wrong financial dealings. (The desire to get ahead and make the most of an opportunity is cunning for us all.)

► The doctor who had been a slave to pornography since early adolescence, and now was an avid advocate of the pro-life movement (a more than worthy cause), but his drivenness was to purge his personal guilt more than to save a life. (How often people do right things with sinfully wrong motivations.)

► The missionary who came to grips with the fact that he was on the field to avoid painful family relationships, while looking for the strokes of doing "God's good work" with such "sacrifice" so far away from home. (A creeping, increasing loneliness finally drove him to the truth.)

► The parachurch worker who realized that he did not need to live in bondage to the overbearing, dysfunctional head of his organization and to a philosophy of ministry that regularly used people up rather than built them up consistently. This person found he could actually leave the group and maintain his salvation, and begin to grow up. (People pleasers are almost always on an unconscious suicide mission that prevents them from enjoying the maturity and freedom they deeply long for.)

▶ The pastor who asked if he and his wife could simply come and have a marital checkup before any cracks did appear in their relationship. (What's that again? That's novel and refreshing, even though not too many are known to be this courageous. For what if something is found out that needs to be dealt with, faced, worked on, as with this couple?)

There is no doubting that our adversary, Satan, is trying to destroy relationships, ministries, people. A war is going on for the heart and mind of every believer. Christian leaders are no exception. If anything, get those leaders out of the way and it's easier to subdue the stunned followers. This is not a new tactic, but we're still caught off guard.

In this past year my heart was heavy over the accounts of those Christian leaders, who, for whatever reason, got caught, were found out, fell again, or forfeited relationships and ministry because of discouragement, burnout, unresolved anger, disillusionment, fear, or not trusting God to be big enough or safe enough to handle their particular pain. This pain came from past or present relationships and circumstances, long-term weariness, no clear focus and direction in both their personal and ministry life, or justified self-righteousness and self-centeredness that led to poor attitudes, defensive words, and noncaring, or unloving behavior. They think they can solve their own issues by themselves (pray harder, do more, change positions or places, memorize more), except those unresolved issues keep showing up in the mind, heart, and lifestyle.

When will you and I learn not to put someone up on a pedestal—even a small pedestal? I know that isn't right and you do too. It's sinful. But of men and women in ministry we do hope for certain authentic lifestyles. Some who have fallen this year *have* been a surprise, and it has been hurtful personally, as well as damaging to the cause of Christ.

However, you and I, living within this sinful shell called a body, have all the potential of falling as long and hard as anyone else. If you say, "Not me," then I shall be most concerned about you first in the months to come.

Each of us is "twenty minutes short" of gross error and sin, if that long. We need to ponder honestly and carefully for our own lives those scriptures that instruct us to deal with the beam in our own eye before getting all concerned about the speck in the eye of another. And Jesus' words still ring true today, "Let he who is without sin cast the first stone."

But let us not use these points of truth to abort looking deep within our own lives and being concerned about the Christian leaders we know. Let us not use our choice words and appropriate actions as fronts for denying that which plagues us in our minds and hearts in our most private moments.

If I were with you at this moment, I would ask you,

- ▶ Where are you struggling in any way in *any* area of *your* life?
- ▶ What have you never told anyone about, that you sometimes work hard at keeping a secret, that could hurt you and those you love, if it were known?
- ▶ What has happened to you in the past that has damaged or hurt you severely and you have never told anyone, to acknowledge it and come to grips with it?
- ▶ What do you believe could destroy you, if it is not addressed, confessed, worked through, understood, and healed?

I would hope that you would not disregard me, or anyone else who might care enough to ask you the toughest of questions. You owe that to yourself, your family, your coworkers, and most of all, to your Lord.

Some Christian leader reading these words will ignore the intent and the content of this letter and fall needlessly into sin this year. It may be just a small step — "Come on, it's nothing serious. After all, nobody's perfect." Or that leader may take a big plunge in a moment of passion or of seeking relief from intense inner pain.

Will it be you?

From the bottom of my heart I hope not.

But it could be you. You are a prime candidate if you consider yourself a Christian leader of any kind.

Relatively few Christian leaders woke up this morning deliberately thinking, *Now, let's see, just how close to the edge can I walk today? What sins can I commit, enjoy, and get away with?*

It's not that simple. Most leaders who get into various levels of trouble have several things in common, no matter what the issue. First, there is little to no accountability in the areas of their personal, private life and in their lifework. What is meant by that word *accountability?* "Accountability: Answering the Hard Questions" is the title to chapter 8 of Chuck Swindoll's book *Living Above the Level of Mediocrity*. His insights bring an excellent definition and focus to much of what good, careful accountability needs to be about.

If a Christian leader rejects or avoids accountability from those who genuinely care, that leader is in trouble in some area of life. Too often the leader will say, "Well, I'm accountable to my spouse." To which I say, "Fine. But that is too much burden for the spouse to carry alone, especially if some area of life is not right and has not been for some time. Who are the two to five people of your own sex to whom you are accountable — no holds barred?" Anything less is inviting trouble to creep up and throw you down.

Second, you can only know what you are told or shown. I've had leaders look me straight in the eye and say, "No, I'm not in trouble. I'm not having an affair. There is no temptation that way," even when I have asked them directly, with evidence, if they are having an affair.

Leaders in trouble lie. They fear the devastation of being found out. They have told themselves that no one will be there for them if they tell the truth. So they lie some more to cover their tracks, which leads to deeper ruts and further desperation and more trying harder, until they fall over from exhaustion and the weight of their sin.

We all have asked the question, "How can *they* (those fallen leaders) have such an effective ministry while being in the midst of gross, hidden, continuing sin?"

Unfortunately, that is an arrogant, awful question that presupposes degrees of sinful activity: one sin is terrible, another sin is not quite so bad. The question also presupposes that the one asking is himself fully open, has no denial, does not hide from his own sinful thoughts, words, and actions. If you know your own heart as the Lord does, you know that is not true at points in your own life. You need look no further about how *they* cover up what is truly going on than how you cover up and go on acting as if all is well, when it is not well in your own life.

We want to believe that what a person is saying or living is the truth. We expect that of our Christian leaders. We want to believe that they are the same in private as in public. Do you expect that of yourself?

Third, leaders in trouble do not have someone outside their marriage, if married, who knows all there is to know about them. Too often, when a leader does dare to be honest and vulnerable and confesses his struggles before "getting caught," confidentiality is not kept.

Do you know of anything faster than the "greased-Christian-gossip grapevine"? I don't. Not in any locale, not nationally, and with today's e-mail, not even internationally. We Christians seem to enjoy too much the dirt and downsides of someone else's life.

We *prayerfully* pass on the news instead of taking great care to find out whether what we heard about a Christian brother or sister is true or not. Too often, if the rumor has any validity, we continue to pass it on. If we find the rumor is not true, our pride may prevent us from going back to those we "prayed" with and telling them the truth. After all, who wants to be wrong. You need to consider how you would feel if someone spoke against you.

This kind of behavior on the part of Christian followers, and leaders, only sows further seeds of doubts that anyone can be trusted. Many Christian leaders have multiple wounds in their past for sharing from their heart their personal issues. They have learned early on to keep it to themselves and struggle on.

Christian leaders are not supposed to have personal problems. Their marriages and families are supposed to be models of perfection. They know all the right ways to avoid temptation. Their leadership is to be faultless. They are to be what the people want them to be. Since they are the "holy ones," why don't they just simply act that way? And that's what often happens; all action and good-sounding words and little feeling and reality. For who can those leaders trust with how they feel, what they think, what they do when they hurt or are discouraged or have done something wrong?

I am not advocating that everyone know everything about everybody. That would not be right. But I am advocating that in the life of every Christian leader, in your life and mine, beyond marriage, who will know everything there is to know? If ever the hidden issues of your life become known, who will stand with you in saying that the issue has been acknowledged? Who will stand with you to say it has been confessed? Who will stand with you to say that the painful but healing process of repentance is in motion? Who will stand with you to say, yes, you are continuing to work on that issue in a manner that is bringing life out of honest brokenness and repentance?

There is a distinct hazard to this ministry of seeing a variety of Christian leaders strengthened in all their relationships at home, in their lifework, and in their leisure. The hazard is in suspecting who is and who isn't telling the truth about how "fine" their life truly is. I'm not the fourth person of the Trinity, and neither are you, but does every Christian leader have secrets, unknown areas of life that are needing to be explored, faced, worked through? I'm beginning to believe that the answer is resoundingly yes!

What about you? What are the areas in your own life that keep causing you to be unsettled, frustrated, burdened, overwhelmed?

Guess what? Whatever those areas are, you are not the only person on the planet with those struggles. You're not even the first. There is hope, if you will be courageous enough to respond. God can be trusted to take you through these hard places because He has come to give you life in the midst of pain, freedom in the midst of fear, and joy in the midst of confusion. Truly His grace is amazing in response to our various sins.

In part, this is why Life Enrichment exists: to walk with you through the weary, wounded, hurting areas of your life. We have a solid, growing network of gifted counselors around North America and throughout the world who are capable of tackling any issue you can imagine. These men and women, who have ministries around the globe, offer a variety of assistance to Christian leaders. It would be a privilege to link you up with one of them, according to your needs. These men and women *will hold* a confidence and not let out any of your issues, whether you are well known or only known to a few.

Contact us before the pain, wrong attitudes, and sinful perspectives get too great. Call, e-mail, fax, or write to us before it is too late for you and those you care about. Our address and numbers are:

Life Enrichment
14581 East Tufts Avenue
Aurora, CO 80015
Office — 303/693-3954
FAX — 303/766-9134
E-mail — CompuServe 103006,3320

Don't become the next statistic of a fallen leader. It isn't necessary, if you have the courage and that is what God wants to give you. We're here for you, where no issue is too small or too large. People are waiting to walk with you through your life. You are not alone.

The phone rang just the other day, and the voice on the other end of the line was familiar. It was a good friend calling. He said he had just resigned his position and that he never thought he would be calling me about a critical personal issue. "Can I come see you as soon as possible or have you get me in touch with someone? I've been covering an area of my life for years. I've lied to you and everyone else I know. I told my family yesterday afternoon and my board last night. I can't hide this any longer. Will you help me?"

Because I had a fairly close friendship with this person, I was numb. "No!" I shouted inside myself, "Not him!"

Yes, even him.

And it could be you who is next. When . . . if . . . we are here for you, too. We know that healing and movement toward wholeness is possible from all that we have been through. God staked His life on it—for you.

BIBLIOGRAPHY

Alban Institute. "The Seven Major Stressors in Ministry." Washington, D.C.:
    The Alban Institute, n.d.

Author unknown. *People Magazine,* 6 April 1992.

Congo, David. "What Causes Burnout." *Theology, News and Notes,* March
    1984.

Gilbert, Barbara. *Who Ministers to Ministers?* Washington, D.C.: Alban
    Institute, 1987.

Ginter, Dian, and Martin, Glen. *Drawing Closer: A Step-By-Step Guide to
    Intimacy with God.* Nashville, Tenn.: Broadman/Holman, 1995.

Ginter, Dian, and Martin, Glen. *Power House: A Step-By-Step Guide to Building
    a Church That Prays.* Nashville, Tenn.: Broadman/Holman, 1994.

Harris, Pierce. Cited in Marshall Shelley, "The Problems of Battered Pastors."
    Christianity Today, 17 May 1985.

Hart, Arch. "Pastor Burnout." *Theology, News and Notes,* March 1984.

Howatch, Susan. *Glittering Images.* New York: Fawcett, 1988.

Manning, Brennan. *Abba's Child.* Colorado Springs, Colo.: NavPress, 1994.

Manning, Brennan. *The Ragamuffin Gospel.* Portland, Oreg.: Multnomah, 1990.

Manning, Brennan. *The Signature of Jesus.* Old Tappan, N.J.: Fleming H.
    Revell, 1988.

Nouwen, Henri. *In the Name of Jesus: Reflections on Christian Leadership.*
    New York: Crossroad Publishing, 1994.

Perotta, Kevin. "Five Advantages of Pastoral Care for Leaders." *Faith &
    Renewal,* November/December 1990.

Peterson, Eugene H. *Five Smooth Stones for Pastoral Work.* Grand Rapids,
    Mich.: Eerdmans, 1992.

Peterson, Eugene H. *The Contemplative Pastor.* Dallas, Tex.: Word Inc., n.d.

Peterson, Eugene H. *Underneath the Unpredictable Plant.* Grand Rapids, Mich.:
    Eerdmans, 1992.

Peterson, Eugene H. *Working the Angles.* Grand Rapids, Mich.: Eerdmans,
    1987.

Riley, Linda. *Esteem Them Highly: Understanding Your Pastor and His Family.*
    Torrance, Calif.: Called Together Ministries, 1987.

Rediger, G. Lloyd. "Clergy Killers." *The Clergy Journal,* August 1993.

Shelley, Marshall. "The Problems of Battered Pastors." *Christianity Today,* 17
    May 1985.

Stanley, Paul, and Clinton, Robert. *Connecting: The Mentoring Relationships
    You Need to Succeed in Life.* Colorado Springs, Colo.: NavPress Publishing
    Group, 1992.

Swindoll, Charles R. *Living Above the Level of Mediocrity.* Dallas, Tex.: Word
    Inc., n.d.

Wagner, Peter. *Prayer Shield.* Ventura, Calif.: Regal Books, 1992.

Whittemore, Hank. "Ministers Under Stress." *Parade Magazine,* 14 April 1991.

AUTHOR

Wes Roberts was born in Oregon in 1942 and raised on a large ranch west of Corvallis on the edge of the coastal foothills. After graduating from a country high school, he headed south for Los Angeles. In 1967, Wes graduated from Biola University with a B.A. in Christian education and a call from God.

Moving into full-time Christian ministry, Wes worked as an associate pastor of youth and families in a growing Baptist church in southern California. In 1973, he and his wife, Judy, moved to Denver, Colorado, where he continued his graduate education at Denver Seminary. Upon completion in 1976, Wes became a minister of counseling at a fast-growing Presbyterian church in the Denver suburbs.

In 1981, Wes felt called by God to minister to Christian leaders—pastors, missionaries, parachurch workers, people in the marketplace and the professions—and encourage them to encounter the incredible and unending grace of Almighty God. Since 1982, he has been the president of Life Enrichment, an organization dedicated to renewing Christian leaders in all areas of their lives.

Wes and Judy have one daughter, Shannon.